THE GREAT FLOOD OF 1937

RISING WATERS – SOARING SPIRITS
LOUISVILLE, KENTUCKY

To: Jo Ann

"Flood Baby"

Rick Bell

1937 Ohio River Flood Photograph Collections – 1986.58.6

THE GREAT FLOOD
OF 1937

RISING WATERS – SOARING SPIRITS
LOUISVILLE, KENTUCKY

RICK BELL

IN ASSOCIATION WITH

THE UNIVERSITY OF LOUISVILLE PHOTOGRAPHIC ARCHIVES

Butler Books

The historic images contained in this book were provided by the following:

From the University of Louisville Libraries, Special Collections:
The Caufield and Shook Collection
The R.G. Potter Collection
The Royal Photo Studio Collection
The 1937 Ohio River Flood Photograph Collections
The Louisville Free Public Library Collection
The Louisville Herald-Post Photographs Collection
The Metropolitan Sewer District (MSD) Collection
The Postcard Collection
Scrapbook of Mayor Neville Miller

From the University of Kentucky, Special Collections and Digital Programs
Goodman-Paxton Photographic Collection, 1934-1942

The Courier-Journal, Louisville, KY

GettyImages

The Collection of Mike Maloney

The Collection of Scott Nussbaum

For more information about images in Special Collections, University of Louisville Libraries, visit the Ekstrom Library,
2301 South Third Street, Belknap Campus, University of Louisville, Louisville, KY 40292;
visit the website: http://library.louisville/ekstrom/special/;
or contact the staff by telephone: 502-852-6752, fax: 502-852-8734, or email: Special.Collections@louisville.edu.

For more information about images in Special Collections and Digital Programs, University of Kentucky, visit
the Audio-Visual Archives, Margaret I. King Library, University of Kentucky, Lexington, KY, 40506-0039;
or contact the staff by telephone: 859-257-2654, or by fax 859-257-6311.

ISBN 1-884532-82-9
Printed in the United States of America

Photo Editor: James E. Manasco
Book Designer: Scott Stortz

For more information, contact the publisher:

Butler Books
P.O. Box 7311, Louisville, KY 40207
502-897-9393/Fax 502-897-9797
www.butlerbooks.com

The Louisville Spirit

As war tests the stamina of a nation and brings out the heroism in human nature,
disaster tests the stamina and resourcefulness of a community. Louisville has made a proud record
throughout the ordeal of the flood situation, and, grateful for the generous aid given its stricken
people by good neighbors far and near, it is going to carry on to bigger and better things,
inspired by its own innate strength.

Louisville people love Louisville, the more for what they have endured together.

Editorial
Courier-Journal
February 6, 1937

PREFACE

Cultures from every part of the earth tell stories about a legendary flood in their past so enormous it changed their world forever. Whether it is Noah's biblical flood in Genesis, the Babylonian Epic of Gilgamesh, or the emergence myth of the Navajos, flood stories provide an elemental way for people to understand each other, and the earth they live upon.

For the people of Louisville, Kentucky, the Great Flood of 1937 is their epic tale of trial by water. In the winter of 1937, the Falls Cities were hammered by a flood of terrifying proportions. During an eighteen-day period of record high water and frigid temperatures, the community rose to new heights of generosity, ingenuity, stamina, and courage. Louisville's darkest moment was also its finest.

A key element of the universal flood myths is that they are remembered and shared with others. One of the most important legacies of Louisville's Great Flood has been the participants' willingness to pass on their experiences to future generations. In so doing, the flood veterans have enriched us with the excellence of their example and the worth of their values.

Like most children growing up in Louisville in the 1950s, I learned about the 1937 Flood while sitting at the evening dinner table, or at family get–togethers. If you grew up in Portland there were daily reminders of the lasting impact left by the Flood on your family, your neighbors and your home. Commemorative markers, high on telephone poles or painted on the sides of buildings, delineated the Flood's highest crest. I remember them being pointed out with a sense of both pride and defiance.

At big family gatherings – and ours is a big family – I recall at an early age asking questions of my aunts and uncles about a particular family story, or a favorite Flood joke. I tried to bring the conversation around, as it so often did, to the Flood and the bittersweet memories. I was always amazed that regular people – like my family – lived such a remarkable adventure.

I began to systematically research the '37 Flood prior to the 50th anniversary of the event and a series of citywide celebrations held in the winter of 1987. Working at The Filson Club, and privy to the sage advice of Executive Director James R. Bentley, I prepared a presentation that focused on the chronology of the Flood. Later that year, Mary Jane Kinsman and I presented an illustrated show, using photographs from the Club's collection, that was enthusiastically received. The 50th anniversary celebrations brought forth new interest in the old Flood and many veterans came forth with their remembrances.

Twenty years later, as the 70th anniversary of the event approaches, far fewer of the '37 Flood veterans are still around to share their stories. Last year, when Hurricane Katrina struck New Orleans, the vivid images of natural and man–made disasters evoked remarkable parallels with Louisville's flood experience. Pictures of desperate people standing on their rooftops, begging to be saved, are too powerful to dismiss. I thought it was time to revisit the Great Flood and tell the old stories once again.

I have been delighted, and a bit amazed, at people's interest when I mentioned the idea of writing a book on the 1937 Flood. The subject touches anyone with roots in the community and many urged me to complete the work prior to the 70th anniversary in January 2007. I must thank those who have encouraged the project. Joanne Weeter, our city's champion of historic preservation, introduced me to Carol and Bill Butler of Butler Books, and the publication was officially on.

The Photographic Archives and Special Collections section of the University of Louisville's Ekstrom Library is a national treasury of visual images, research opportunities and historic ephemera. Their uncommonly rich collection, over 1.75 million photographic images, is surpassed only by the excellence of its caretakers. James E. Manasco, Head of Collection Development and Coordinator of Operations, Special Collections, recognized the potential for a major retrospective study of the 1937 Flood and became an eager contributor to the project.

Professor Delinda Buie, Curator of Rare Books, added her wisdom and encouragement to the entire process. Staff assistance included Imaging by Amy Hanaford Purcell, Associate Curator; Rachel I. Howard, Digitization Librarian; and Bill Carner, Library Specialist. Virtually all of the photographs included in the book are drawn from UofL Libraries' extensive Photo Archives in Special Collections.

The Special Collections department introduced me to a researcher's dream, the Flood Scrapbook of Mayor Neville Miller. Stuffed with original photos, newspaper clippings from around the world, and occasional editorial comments in the Mayor's handwriting, the large fragile scrapbook provided fresh insight into the entire flood crisis with special emphasis on the Mayor's remarkable personal contributions.

Several friends came to my aid, as friends always do, when it came to reading the painful first draft. Chuck Parrish, historian for the U.S. Corps of Engineers, shared both his files and his keen perception, honed through 30 years of intelligent research into the Falls of the Ohio. His comments and reminders were invaluable.

Lynn Howard, a skilled wordsmith, saved me from embarrassment, and readers from confusion. Her keen editorial eye, and an appreciative ear for storytelling, went a long way toward producing clarity to the sometimes confusing chronology of the Flood.

Very special thanks go to Mike Maloney, connoisseur of all things Louisville, for his insightful observations and genuine enthusiasm for the project. I most especially thank him for sharing the letters and diaries of his grandmothers, Elinor Maloney and Helen Hamilton Magers. Their words ring true, in both their optimism and their fears, and vividly remind us of their trials and their triumphs.

One of the highlights of the research process was an afternoon when Mike and I traced, through old photographs, the actual path of the floating Pontoon Bridge. For two guys fascinated with Louisville's heritage, it was like discovering the source of the Nile.

As always, I thank my wife Susie for sharing our adventure together. From the Seelbach's Rathskeller, to the Great Sage Plains, Susie sets the highest standards and is never afraid to live life fully. For Walking in Beauty with me, all I can do is give thanks.

My greatest debt goes to those with whom I first sat at the dinner table, and who shared their stories of a remarkable time in Louisville. *This book is dedicated to my parents Dorothy and Fred Bell, and my brother Russell.*

INTRODUCTION

This is the story of the Great Flood of 1937. The event was an unparalleled national disaster affecting millions of Americans and causing unprecedented destruction. Its greatest wrath was visited upon the citizens of Louisville, Kentucky. The 1937 Flood – the most serious crisis in the city's history – defined Louisville's character more than any other experience.

The Great Flood at Louisville was a part of a much larger event, the Ohio–Mississippi Valley floods of 1937. The floods of 1937 were the greatest natural disaster in our nation's history until that time, causing over 500 deaths and 400 million dollars (nearly 5.4 billion in today's dollars) in damages. Of all the hundreds of cities and towns affected, and of all the millions of lives threatened, no community suffered as greatly as the communities at the Falls of the Ohio – Louisville, New Albany, Clarksville and Jeffersonville.

To understand how totally Louisville was impacted by the Great Flood, consider these figures: of the 64,000 houses in the city, nearly 34,000 were flooded. Over 270 of the city's 350 miles of paved roads were inundated, and 70 percent of the citizens (over 175,000 individuals) were evacuated from their homes. No Louisvillian, from those in the finest mansions in Glenview to the poorest shanty boat in Shippingport, was unaffected by the Great Flood. The 1937 Flood, to those who lived through the experience, was a period of danger, discomfort and deprivation.

Stories from the '37 Flood provide central elements in Louisville's emergence myth: the famous floating Pontoon Bridge which provided an escape route for 75,000 weary refugees; the heroic "Send a Boat" messages from WHAS radio; or a legendary fish caught in the lobby of the Brown Hotel.

Throughout the Great Flood, people demonstrated their genius for survival and every small success was a cause for celebration. The longevity of the crisis – the Ohio River stood above flood stage for 18 consecutive days – provided uncounted opportunities for personal heroism and acts of ingenuity. Two attributes, uncommon bravery and personal resourcefulness, were the hallmarks of Louisvillians during the 1937 Flood.

The more tangible legacies of the 1937 Flood were Louisville's spirit of community and the shared pride people felt in answering their common challenge. It has become accepted practice in recent years to refer to the Americans who fought and won World War II as the "Greatest Generation." In Louisville, the "Greatest Generation" went through Boot Camp during the Great Flood of 1937.

Rising Waters: Every 50 Years

Louisville's history is uniquely tied to the Ohio River. The city was founded in response to the navigational barrier presented by the Falls of the Ohio, a two–mile series of bedrock limestone rapids where the river descends 26 feet in elevation. To bypass this obstruction, boats heading down river stopped and unloaded in Louisville and were forced to transport cargo and passengers around the Falls to Portland or Shippingport. The city's economy has always been identified with river industries, and Louisville continues to be one of America's great inland port cities.

The site of the city of Louisville is located on low and undulating ground. Most of Louisville's West End is surrounded on three sides by the Ohio River, and only the eastern–most section of the city stands significantly above the normal river level. Throughout history, water has risen above flood stage on the average of once every seven years. Approximately every 50 years the city has been invaded by major flooding.

Louisville's river level is measured at the 26th Street gauge located at the Portland Canal. A measurement of 28 feet on that gauge constitutes a flood stage; the level where the Ohio River begins to leave its banks and invade living areas. Eclipsing all other floods in recorded history, the Great Flood of 1937

would reach 57.15 feet, more than 29 feet above flood stage.

The first major flood in local recorded history occurred in 1774, during Kentucky's early frontier period. Although no system of measurement was available to the pioneers, most of the city's future site was inundated at that time.

The next significant flood was in February 1832. The river rose to a crest of 41 feet, about 13 feet above the 28–foot flood stage. A less significant flood in 1861 was a mere preview of the destruction that would visit the city during the 1880s. In a rare set of meteorological circumstances, three consecutive years produced record flooding. In 1882, 1883 and 1884, the river rose above its normal levels and the city suffered considerable damage. The flood of 1884 reached the height of 46.7 feet and would remain the highest recorded measurement of flood waters until 1937.

The winter of 1913 saw a major local flood caused by a slow–moving low–pressure system that deposited 11.41 inches of rain during January. Runoff caused every major river and stream in Kentucky to flood and the U.S. Weather Bureau described the area as a "vast inland sea." The high water crest of 44.9 made it the greatest flood since 1884.

A memorable flood in 1933 reached a crest of 39.1 feet, about

DOOMED!

THE WILD WAVES WILL SHOW NO QUARTER.

AND THE FALLS CITIES ARE AT THE FLOODS MERCY.

THE RIVER COMES UP WITH A RUSH AND A ROAR.

THIRTY SIX FEET AND EIGHT INCHES BY THE MARKS AT MIDNIGHT.

THE GREAT FLOOD OF 1883 TO BE ECLIPSED IN 1884.

GREAT CONSTERNATION IN PORTLAND AND SHIPPINGPORT.

THE LUCKLESS PEOPLE OF THE POINT AGAIN DESERT THEIR HOMES.

THE WATER EXPECTED MOMENTARILY TO DASH OVER THE CUT OFF.

Louisville Commercial - Feb. 3, 1884

The 1884 Flood's crest of 46.7 feet stood as the high water standard in Louisville for over 50 years. Standing at Shelby Street and looking east on Broadway, street car rails disappear into the overflowing waters of the Ohio River and Beargrass Creek. The crest of the 1937 Flood would exceed the record 1884 mark by more than ten feet.

R.G. Potter Collection – 536

"...that rare combination of events which is favorable to the creation of a 'super flood' in the Ohio River."

Report of the Chief Hydraulic Engineer, Department of the Interior, 1938

five–and–a–half feet below the 1913 standard. Flooding reached low–lying residential areas that routinely flooded, and volunteers came forth to sandbag buildings, transport refugees and pump wet basements. City officials took notice and began to upgrade communications equipment and rescue vehicles. The flood of 1933 would provide an excellent training exercise for what was to come four years later.

Fulton Street was located in the old Point neighborhood, the area stretching east on River Road from the Fourth Street Wharf to the Cut–Off Bridge. During the 1933 Flood, city officials erected sandbag dikes to help control the rising waters. This view looks west down Fulton Street from the intersection with Ohio Street and toward the Big Four Bridge.

Metropolitan Sewer District Collection – O.R.F. 34

Things went terribly awry with America's weather during the 1930s. The year 1936 began with the Ohio River freezing in January, only to be followed in six months by the hottest summer of the 20th Century. America's midsection was gripped by its third visitation of the Great Drought that produced the Dust Bowl. Locally, two major floods occurred between March 1936 and February 1937. In summarizing the cause of the 1937 Flood, the official Report of Relief Operations of the American Red Cross provided perspective on the origin of the epic disaster in the Ohio and Mississippi river valleys:

Official Report of Relief Operations of the American Red Cross
1937 Flood, Louisville, Ky

Within one month from the middle of December, 1936, this important, populous, wealthy region was to know devastation without parallel in the history of the United States.

Then it was that United States Weather Bureau observers began to note a peculiar atmospheric condition. Since the beginning of the month, abnormal cold had persisted in the Pacific States, the Plateau and Rocky Mountain regions, the Plains States, and, at times, the upper Mississippi Valley.

The area of cold (high pressure) failed to rotate as customary, toward the east. It hung stationary, as though too dense and heavy to move. Off the Eastern Coast, another wall of cold hovered over the Bahamas and Bermuda.

Flowing northward between these two freezing barriers came tropical air masses, saturated with water. As the warm air met the cold, the clouds dropped their burden which totaled 165,000,000,000 tons of rain before this strange month in the history of weather reporting came to an end.

No, this was not a repetition of the Mississippi Flood of 1927. This was worse. This was a disaster attacking man where he was most vulnerable – in urban centers where human beings live crowded together. No respecter of persons, the flood afflicted poor, middle class and rich alike.

The Ohio-Mississippi Valley Flood of 1937 possibly lends itself too easily to the use of superlatives. Undoubtedly, next to the World War, it was from the standpoint of human suffering, destruction of property, and cost, the worst disaster in the history of the nation.

To call it "the greatest disaster" is perhaps not only an inadvisable use of the adjective "great" but a dangerous practice as well. One of the outstanding obstacles to rescue work at certain points along the Ohio was the belief that the 1913 flood was the "greatest" and that therefore the waters would not rise beyond the stage registered in that year.

The difficulties of superlatives in connection with disasters are illustrated by the following statement in the official Red Cross report of the Mississippi Valley Flood of 1927: "…the Mississippi Valley Flood stands out as the greatest disaster this country has ever suffered. It ranks, in fact, well among the great natural catastrophes of the world's history."

Yet the Ohio-Mississippi Valley Flood was nearly twice as big!

During a minor river rise during 1924, businesses at the foot of Fourth Street were inundated. At that time, a railroad spur transversed the old Louisville Wharf, where today I–64 moves streams of vehicular traffic east and west. In Louisville's earlier days, this block of Fourth Street stretching from Main Street north to the river was known as Wall Street.

Caufield and Shook Collection – 54008

The most commonly asked question concerning the 1937 Flood is, "What caused it?" It is also one of the most easily answered. It rained. It rained in historic quantities and it rained day after day. In January 1937 the city recorded an amazing 19.17 inches of rainfall, about half of the normal annual average precipitation. During the five–day period of January 20 through 24, the city received 10.3 inches of rain, plus several additional inches of snow and driving sleet.

At this time there were no systems of flood control – no floodwalls or levees, no reservoirs on the tributaries or any engineering improvements to the Ohio River. The water pouring into Louisville's river, streams and creeks had nowhere to go. The great storms of January 1937 also occurred to the north and east of Louisville, and all that excess rain swelled the Ohio River and rushed downstream.

"Trouble is," said an old Cincinnati water–front man, "lots of this land where houses are really always has belonged to the river…People just keep encroaching on the river, with mills and warehouses and wharves, making them narrower and narrower. Then, when it gets high and must spread, there's no place for it to spread except up into somebody's second–story windows."

National Geographic, 1937

The City of Louisville and Jefferson County of 1937 were dramatically different communities than today. At that time about 325,000 people lived within the city limits, most in rather close proximity to the Ohio River. The bulk of the population lived west of downtown, or in the central business district. In 1937, only 17,820 citizens lived in rural Jefferson County. The flood waters covered 76 square miles of Jefferson County and would destroy or disrupt most of the 3,288 farms. Today, with a merged city and the new city of Louisville Metro is the home of 700,000 residents.

In 1937 the city claimed an excess of 64,000 houses, with the median value being $4,650. The average monthly rental on a Louisville house in 1937 was $23.26. The busiest street corner in town was Fourth and Walnut (today's Muhammad Ali Blvd.). In a 12–hour period during one 1937 weekday, 68,831 people were counted passing through this intersection.

Louisville, like the rest of the United States, was slowly recovering from the devastating effects of the Stock Market Crash of 1929 and the Great Depression. The city was experiencing sound industrial expansion and the attitude of civic leaders was generally optimistic and progressive. The year 1933 had marked the bottom of the Depression in Louisville, and by 1935 the value of local industrial output reached an all–time peak of over $277,000,000. At the start of 1935 there were 568 industrial plants in the city, 49 more than just two years before. By 1936 the economic picture was even brighter with the establishment of 14 new industries and enlargement of 72 older plants. More Louisvillians were working and earning better incomes. Jobs for white collar workers were increasing as dramatically as those for laborers.

Life in Louisville was like most of America in 1937. Newspaper accounts and Movietone News reports from around the nation and the world recorded popular culture and fashions. *Gone With The Wind* won the Pulitzer Prize for fiction; Amelia Earhart vanished over the Pacific Ocean; King Edward VIII abdicated his throne to marry his American girlfriend, Wallace Simpson, and Walt Disney released his first full–length animated film *Snow White and the Seven Dwarfs*. The Golden Gate Bridge was completed and Frank Lloyd Wright built "Fallingwater" in Pennsylvania.

Locally, the first shipment of gold bullion reached the newly–constructed Fort Knox Depository in mid–January. In May, the great racehorse War Admiral would win the Kentucky Derby, but this achievement was overshadowed, as it occurred on the day before the dirigible "Hindenburg" exploded in New Jersey.

"The flood of 1937 seems to have been the jolt that awoke Louisville.
Like San Francisco's earthquake and Baltimore's fire, the flood became
a local benchmark. Modern Louisville started with it."

Harper's Magazine
August 1955

Louisville's Fourth Street was alive with pedestrians, traffic and commerce following World War I. The city's major hotels, restaurants, clothiers and theaters lined the street from Broadway north to Main Street. The corner of Main and Liberty streets, anchored by the Will Sales Building, served the central business district and its complexes of legal, medical and government offices.

Caufield and Shook Collection – 167356

Ironically, optimism was prevalent for the first time in years throughout the empire of the Ohio basin. Except in the long depressed old river towns, business was on the upturn at last. Factories were humming in Evansville and Louisville. Cincinnati was regaining its economic feet. West Virginia's steel was traveling east in heavy train loads.

Cheerfully industrious again, the valley seemed to have recaptured the spirit of the days when the river was the broad water highway to the West. Back in the early 1800s, cheap water transportation had made thriving cities of the trading posts. Later, with the beginning of the industrial era, manufactories were built close to the landings (and so were the homes of the workers).

Red Cross Report, 1937

"People just keep encroaching on the river"

In their pioneering stages, the original six communities known collectively as the Falls Cities – Louisville, Shippingport and Portland on the Kentucky side, and Jeffersonville, Clarksville and New Albany on the Indiana shore – made proximity to the Ohio River their highest priority. The commerce of each of the independent towns was based upon the river, with boat manufacturing, milling or trans–shipping as the basis of their economy. Waterside locations were eagerly sought as prime sites for warehouses, taverns, hotels, and chandleries.

Historian George Yater perceptively observed that the river made Louisville a town, but the steamboat made Louisville a city. Shortly after Captain Henry Miller Shreve, a Portland ferryboat operator, brought the first steamboat upriver from New Orleans in 1815, a new era of prosperity and opportunity gripped the Falls Cities.

Proximity to the river was a double–edged sword. Commerce was dependent upon the river trade and in the era before mass transit, workers lived near their work and owners near their businesses. Residential neighborhoods developed on the banks of creeks and the river. Among the earliest permanent settlements at the Falls were Shippingport, Portland, Beargrass Creek and the "Point". Each area is adjacent to a flood plain, and throughout local history, each location has been among the earliest areas to suffer inundation.

The "Point" and Beargrass Creek

Few people today remember the area known as the "Point" as a distinctive neighborhood. While not many recognize the name, thousands of people drive through the Point every day, and throngs enjoy the manicured lawns and recreational opportunities provided by Waterfront Park. While the area is now one of great local pride, the residential neighborhood known as the Point enjoyed a less savory reputation.

When George Rogers Clark and his party first arrived at the Falls of the Ohio in 1778, his small flotilla pulled into the Kentucky shore at Beargrass Creek. At that time, Beargrass Creek entered the Ohio River between Third and Fourth streets. Today, the Belle of Louisville docks at this location. Three forks of Beargrass Creek span eastern Jefferson County like a spider web and drain the low hills that form the Highlands. These three forks merge near the old Bourbon Stock Yards in Butchertown. Newcomers to Louisville are often surprised to

The gentle meandering streams that form the three forks of Beargrass Creek have charmed local artists and photographers for decades. During major flood events, Beargrass Creek can change into a raging torrent, splitting downtown Louisville from the safer, elevated neighborhoods in the Highlands or Crescent Hill.
Herald-Post – 0826

Beargrass Creek near Schiller cuts through the eastern section of the Germantown neighborhood. Throughout history, whenever the Ohio River rises above flood stage, the tributaries of Beargrass Creek begin to leave their banks.

R.G. Potter Collection – 6530

learn that the gentle and elegant creeks adjacent to Seneca and Cherokee parks are capable of raging out of their banks and invading homes.

Beargrass Creek had long attracted pioneers in flatboats as a safe harbor, but Louisville's waterfront became valuable wharf space during the 1840s. On some days, 30 or more steamboats tied up at this location while loading and unloading.

The narrow wedge of land that started at Third Street and ran eastward between the Ohio River and Beargrass Creek became known as the "Point". By the 1850s, the expense and inconvenience of bridging downtown streets to span Beargrass Creek convinced local leaders that the entire channel should be diverted and filled. In 1854 Beargrass Creek was relocated to enter the Ohio at the Cut–Off Bridge, on River Road just east of Frankfort Avenue.

The Point's proximity to the Ohio River produced a rough–and–tumble community that accommodated rowdy boatmen and ignored the disapproval of local bluebloods. Low–rent grog shops and houses of ill fame dotted the Point during its heyday. The area was the home of heavy industries involved in

In 1854 the natural course of Beargrass Creek was diverted from its original outlet near Fourth Street, and moved to enter the Ohio River upstream on River Road just east of Frankfort Avenue. The Cut–Off Bridge allowed passage between River Road and the area adjacent to the river called the "Point." A neighborhood of river people and small businesses, the Point would be one of the first casualties of the 1937 Flood.

Herald-Post – 0105

Louisville 1853 map –Published by I.H. Colton & Co. No. 172 William St New York

boiler–making, engine construction, tanneries and boatyards. In later years, scrap yards and garbage dumps predominated.

Although people of leisure located their summer cottages at Turner Park, on the Point's eastern edge, and kept their boats at fashionable boat clubs, as a neighborhood the area was in solid decline. By the mid–1930s approximately 75 families lived more–or–less permanently, depending upon the river level, between Tow Head Island and downtown. Some were shanty–boaters, folks who lived in floatable houses with no foundations, no electricity and no plumbing.

Throughout its history, people had returned to the Point even though every flood proved devastating. Local newspaper accounts during the epic floods of the 1880s are replete with tales of heroic rescues, starving populations and local charities straining to assist suffering "Pointers". The Great Flood of 1937 would end these concerns and the Point, as a residential neighborhood, for good.

"Oh law Gals, don't you want to go to Shippingport?*"

By 1806, the community originally chartered as "Anonymous, Kentucky" was being called Shippingport. Founded by elegant French émigrés like the Tarascons and Berthouds, the community on the northern–most point of land at the Falls of the Ohio became one of the American West's first boom–towns. Symbolized by the massive water–powered Tarascon Mill, Shippingport was the first town to attempt to harness the power of the Falls.

Shippingport, with its inviting small harbor formed between the main shore and Sand Island, was the original landing place for boats below the Falls. This lively French community played host to famous visitors like Aaron Burr, and local shopkeeper John James Audubon and his wife Lucy. Shippingport exuded confidence in itself and its future, but the town's site would prove its eventual undoing.

Popular agitation to build a canal around the Falls navigational barrier began soon after the first pioneer landed. Numerous schemes, promotions, lotteries and bond sales were hatched to finance a canal and lock system on either the

As illustrated in these *Courier–Journal* woodcuts from the 1898 Flood, the old town of Shippingport was one of the first local areas to flood. Once a thriving community of French immigrants, Shippingport became one of America's first Western 'ghost–towns." The town achieved commercial success during the 1820s in the early days of steam boating, but dramatically declined after the digging of the Louisville–Portland Canal and the historic Flood of 1832.

Kentucky or Indiana shore. By 1825, deals were signed and planning begun for the construction on the giant Louisville–Portland Canal. While the original canal would not be completed until 1830, and was far too narrow for most steamboats, its construction doomed the independent town of Shippingport. When the great ditch was completed, Shippingport became a man–made island with its approaches limited to two inadequate bridges that disrupted boat traffic and impeded transportation of cargo and passengers.

In 1832, Louisville's first great flood of the historic era swept across the Falls and virtually destroyed Shippingport. Gone was the local "Bois de Boulogne" with all its French charm. Shippingport descended in social status and by the 1930s the town was in shambles, occupied by only a few dozen old–timers, fishermen and shanty–boaters.

Shippingport's strategic location, jutting out into the rapids of the Ohio, attracted every flood and high water condition. Shippingport's once bright future was past.

* 19th Century minstrel show song

LOUISVILLE COMMERCIAL

17 February 1883

The flood attained its greatest depth in Portland yesterday at noon, measuring seventy—one feet and two inches (lower gauge). This exceeds by six feet the flood of 1832. The scenes in Shippingport and Happy Hollow yesterday were pictures of desolation and despair. The few houses that have withstood the tide were floating around in the water, many of them containing much valuable furniture and other effects. The destitute are being kindly cared for, and almost every family is sheltering some unfortunate neighbor.

A Commercialist made rueful inquiry last night about the probable losses in Portland and Shippingport, with the following results:

Damage to houses in Shippingport, $150,000. Loss of furniture, $20,000. Speed's Cement Mills have been damaged $15,000 and Belknap's Cement Mills have sustained a loss of $20,000. The Illinois Leather Company estimates their loss at $10,000. In Happy Hollow the total damages to houses and property will reach $25,000. The canal authorities place their loss by breaks, etc at $40,000.

All of the houses in the flooded districts remain in about the same condition as they were the day before, with the exception of a few small houses on the Point, which received considerable shaking up from the high wind which blew rather hard about 4 o'clock.

Portland 'Proper'

"When the home of an American is carried down the river,
he builds himself another."

Anthony Trollope, 1862
North America

In 1811, when General William Lytle first established his new town just below Shippingport, he called the community Portland 'Proper'. Six years later he would enlarge his land development to create Portland Avenue, which joined Louisville's Main Street at 13th Street. While he originally wanted to raise enough money to personally build a canal around the Falls, General Lytle also created Louisville's most distinctive and independent neighborhood.

Often elegant, and usually boisterous, Portland came of age during the palmy days of the American steamboat. From its beginning Portland cultivated, protected and relied on its strong sense of identity as a self–contained immigrant community. Immigrants from France, Ireland, Germany and Switzerland, along with African–Americans – free and slave – brought their native languages, customs, skills and personalities to this spot and created new and uniquely American homes and institutions.

Portland reached its pinnacle during the 1840s and '50s and in its glory boasted the grand St. Charles Hotel, the United States Marine Hospital, the Portland Opera House and other impressive structures. Portland's manufacturers produced boilers, axes, whiskey, furniture, shoes, paint, wrought iron, bricks, cement and Pilcher brand organs. Boat stores, confectionaries, warehouses and taverns lined Portland's Water Street wharf. The town's biggest attraction stood on Commercial Street and was the home and tavern belonging to James D. Porter, internationally known as the Kentucky Giant, the tallest man in the world.

Floods routinely poured over Portland's streets and into second–story windows. Portland people learned to adapt and clung to the river's edge despite the sure knowledge they would have to rebuild. In Portland, the river was both a friend and an enemy, and this relationship challenged and confounded generations. In mid–January 1937, the river renewed its enemy status to Portlanders, and soon, all other Louisvillians.

In 1861, the great English novelist Anthony Trollope visited Louisville and left his vivid remembrance of a relatively minor event in Louisville's history, the Flood of 1861.

While I was at Louisville the Ohio was flooded. It had begun to rise when I was at Cincinnati, and since then had gone on increasing hourly, rising inch by inch up into the towns upon its bank. I visited two suburbs of Louisville, both of which were submerged, on the streets and ground–floors of the houses. At Shipping Port, one of these suburbs, I saw the women and children clustering in the up–stairs room, while the men were going about in punts and wherries, collecting driftwood from the river for their winter's firing. In some places bedding and furniture had been brought over to the high ground, and the women were sitting, guarding their little property. That village, amidst the waters, was a sad sight to see; but I heard no complaints. There was no tearing of hair and no gnashing of teeth; no bitter tears or moans of sorrow. The men who were not at work in the boats stood loafing about in clusters, looking at the still rising river; but each seemed to be personally indifferent to the matter. When the home of an American is carried down the river, he builds himself another; — as he would get himself a new coat when his old coat becomes unserviceable. But he never laments or moans such a loss. Surely there is no other people so passive under personal misfortune!

North America, by Anthony Trollope
Vol. 2, 1862: London–Chapman & Hall

"The first day of the flood was the most exciting day of my life."

Jane Rolli
Shawnee High School student

January 15–20, 1937

Following an unusually warm December, rain began falling in Louisville on January 6, 1937. Intermittent rainfall for the next two weeks caused the river to rise. On January 14, a heavy rain of 2.7 inches brought the river level up to 23 feet – five feet below flood stage. The next day River Road between Fourth and Sixth streets was closed to traffic because of high water, and creeks began to leave their banks. The river reached the 28–foot flood stage at 11 p.m. January 15 and continued its rise at a rate of .2 foot an hour.

People began evacuating the flood–prone fishing and boating camps adjacent to the river. Families living in the Point and in Shippingport prepared to leave their homes. A maximum flood stage of 30 feet was predicted by weather forecasters. On January 17 the river briefly began to fall, but a 1.5 inch rain caused the river to rise again immediately.

Meteorologist J. L. Kendall predicted the crest would occur on Sunday, with readings two–and–one–half feet above flood stage. His prediction was based on his observation that the high water on the Ohio did not extend above Cincinnati and there was no snow melt to provide run off. Mr. Kendall also added that no additional major rainfall was expected in the area. He would be proven terribly wrong.

While the river remained stationary for five hours, heavy rains in Cincinnati began to form a crest that moved downriver towards Louisville. On January 18 water had flooded parts of Dixie Highway to a depth of eight feet in some locations. Shawnee Park was closed due to high water and areas of Cherokee Park adjacent to Beargrass Creek were submerged.

On Tuesday, January 19, meteorologists predicted that the flood would crest at nine feet above flood stage, passing the previous year's March flood with its 36.6–foot crest. River Road was blocked from the Standard Club to above Pipeline Lane (Zorn Avenue) and U.S. 31–W was obstructed at West Point. By the end of the day the entire 981–mile length of the Ohio River, from Pittsburgh to Cairo, rose above flood stage.

All residents of the Point were ordered to evacuate. East of the Cut–Off Bridge, 23 families were evacuated by the County Welfare Department, the County Police, and the County Engineer's office. County Patrolman Emile Marrillia and Tom Young of the County Engineering Department worked for 48 consecutive hours coaxing Point residents out of their second story refuges and into boats.

The flood had already forced many to relocate. As usual, the first areas to flood were the last areas dry. Refugees from these areas would be out of their homes for three or more weeks, and many would never return to their waterlogged houses.

U.S. Meteorologist J. L. Kendall monitored the Ohio River's rise upstream in Cincinnati and felt little concern for a major flood in Louisville. His prediction of no significant rainfall proved to be tragically wrong, as over ten inches would fall between January 18 and 21, 1937. Following the Flood, Kendall's analysis of the cause and effect of the weather event was thoroughly professional and provides true insight into the causes of the natural disaster.

Herald Post – 2394

By January 20 the river had reached eight feet above flood stage and an additional 1.7 inches of rain fell. Water blocked virtually all county roads and shut down most vehicle traffic. County roads barricaded included Gardiner's Lane, Bashford Manor, Shuff Lane, Johnson Lane, Watson Lane, Stites Lane, Catherine Road, Fairmount Road, Conn Mill Road, Mockingbird Valley Road, Lime Kiln Road, Blankenbaker Lane and Indian Trail. Families adjoining Beargrass Creek were evacuated. In the south central part of downtown water had covered the corner of 14th and Oak streets and police lines were set up to keep sightseers out of the affected areas.

On January 20, the city set up the first of two relief stations to

provide food, shelter and medical treatment to citizens. The first was established in the assembly room of the Portland Branch Library for the West End, and the second was at the City Incinerator for East End residents.

By this time the city was bracing for a real crisis, with administrators, police and firemen working long hours to control the deteriorating situation. People were transported from flooded areas in government–and privately–owned trucks. An improvement in the design of American vehicles in the mid–1930s – the placement of the carburetor on top of the engine rather than below – allowed many vehicles to continue to operate in several feet of water. In addition, the city used private sport boats and the john–boats of commercial fishermen to carry people out of the flooded areas.

During the 1930s, it was not unusual to see cows in the Portland, Shawnee or Parkland neighborhoods. Many families still kept their milk cow in the shed, and cattle were fattened on the slops from West End distilleries. In the early days of the '37 Flood, wandering cows found relative safety in Shawnee Park, until the entire riverside city park was completely inundated.

R.G. Potter Collection – 535

Ever–increasing rain amounts caused Beargrass Creek to swarm out of its banks and invade Cherokee and Seneca parks. Some of Louisville's most prestigious residential neighborhoods share Beargrass Creek's meandering presence, and usually the scene is appreciated. During flood conditions, the stream forms dangerous barriers to travel and homes.

1937 Ohio River Flood Photograph Collections – 1986.65.04

The corner of First Street and Breckenridge displays the rapidly spreading waters of the flooded Ohio River. Boats soon replaced cars and trucks as the sole means of transportation. One mile south of the river, Breckinridge Street was flooded when the sewer system was overwhelmed and began backing up and filling city streets.

Caufield and Shook Collection – 149506

In the area that would later come to be known as Old Louisville, the 1937 Flood sent waters into the streets surrounding Central Park. This photo, taken on the corner of Fourth and Magnolia streets, shows a high brick wall that still stands. City officials blocked streets to keep sightseers away from scenes of emergency evacuations.

1937 Ohio River Flood Photograph Collections – 1986.56.04

The basement assembly room of the Portland Branch of the Louisville Free Public Library was set up as the first emergency relief center to serve citizens of the West End. The relief center for East End residents was established at the City Incinerator. These initial rescue stations provided meals, shelter and medical attention, but would soon be forced to re–locate when their sites became inaccessible due to rising waters.

Louisville Free Public Library Collection – 1992.18.051

The "Flood Mayor"

Neville Miller was elected mayor of Louisville in 1933, at the depth of the Great Depression. His imaginative and energetic leadership transformed Louisville government through modernization and progressive ideas. The first dean of the Law School at the University of Louisville, Miller's executive decisions prior to the 1937 Flood enhanced public health and safety during the crisis.

Herald Post – 2762

Neville Miller (1894-1977)

After his term as mayor, Neville Miller served as president of the National Association of Broadcasters from 1938 until 1944. He was instrumental in organizing the radio industry during World War II. In 1944, he was named Senior Deputy Chief of the Balkan Mission of the United National Relief and Rehabilitation Association. After the War, Neville Miller opened a private law firm in Washington, D. C., specializing in communications issues. Throughout his career, he drew upon the hard-earned lessons learned directing relief efforts during Louisville's Great Flood of 1937.

While the river continued its dramatic rise, the Governor of Kentucky and the Mayor of Louisville were out of the state. They, like a great many elected officials, were in Washington, D.C. attending the rain–drenched second inauguration of Franklin D. Roosevelt. Governor A. B. "Happy" Chandler, and Mayor Neville Miller would return to their homes, and official duties, and face a crisis greater than any of their predecessors in office.

Both Chandler and Miller were young progressive Democrats, elected to office during the hurricane of political activity that characterized the first term of President Roosevelt. Neville Miller, the son of a prominent Louisville judge, was educated at Princeton and Harvard and served as the University of Louisville's first law school dean. Elected in November 1933, Neville Miller was the first Democrat in fifteen years to serve as Mayor of Louisville.

Neville Miller promised "New Deal" programs to benefit all citizens of Louisville. His hard–fought campaign against Republican Dan Carrell depended upon heavy voting support from the African–American community. Miller was elected with a 3,173 plurality out of 128,000 votes. Typical of the times, at Miller's inauguration in Memorial Auditorium, despite their critical support, the new mayor's African–American backers were assigned to segregated seating on the left side of the balcony.

Miller brought new ideas, energy and direction to a city that had survived the twin economic blows of Prohibition and the Great Depression. Louisville, with much of its economy dependent upon distilling and brewing, was particularly impacted by the legislative experiment known as Prohibition. In 1933, Louisville was a community in need of a visionary leader and it found one in Neville Miller. During his campaign, Miller articulated his goals:

> "I SHALL DEVOTE MY ENTIRE TIME AND ENERGY TO THE AFFAIRS OF THE CITY. WITH THAT PURPOSE IN VIEW I SHALL ENDEAVOR TO SECURE THE HELP OF THE BEST AVAILABLE MEN AND WOMEN IN THE CITY TO ASSIST ME, AND SHALL PUT INTO EFFECT SUCH CHANGES IN THE GOVERNMENT AND POLICIES AS SHALL GIVE TO THE CITIZENS AN HONEST AND EFFICIENT GOVERNMENT."

Mayor Miller kept his promises. One of his first official acts was to call in qualified advisers and initiate an audit and survey of every department of government. Miller's volunteer advisory committee produced over 50 sets of recommendations for improvement of local government. In a remarkable display of political skill, Neville Miller cut costs by 25 percent, removed health and welfare departments from political influence, declared independence from state legislative control, obtained lower utility rates, extended equal protection and access to services for African–Americans, and reorganized the fire and police departments.

Some of the reforms he instituted would pay great dividends during the 1937 Flood. The city budget of 1935 included a new police radio transmitting station, two–way radio communication in police cars, an addition of 40 new police cars, and increased pay. A pioneering advocate of modern radio equipment, Miller opened a new fire headquarters and fire alarm office to enhance communications. He reorganized the Welfare Department to produce more equity in services to African–Americans and increase efficiency of operations.

Mayor Miller received a salary of $5,000 a year for heading a corporation spending $15,000,000 a year. In normal times he worked an 18–hour day, but during the flood crisis he rarely left City Hall, the central command post for rescue and relief. Generations of Louisvillians would remember Neville Miller by his signature local moniker, the "Flood Mayor."

Mayor Miller (on right) is shown at a swearing–in ceremony attended by former Governor Ruby Laffoon (in center). Steady, inspirational and energetic, Mayor Miller directed all governmental relief agencies and served as Provost Marshal after the declaration of Martial Law. Revered by citizens for his irreplaceable leadership during the 1937 natural disaster, generations of Louisvillians would remember Miller as the "Flood Mayor."

Herald Post – 2781

"It can't happen here."

Crews evacuating homes and businesses used City Sanitation trucks as rising waters invaded residential and commercial buildings. Temporary employees of the Works Progress Administration (WPA) made invaluable contributions to flood relief efforts. Very quickly, evacuation became the duty of skilled boatman, and WPA personnel provided experience crews.

Goodman–Paxton – Box 30 Item 4776

Many residents delayed evacuation of their homes until water was ready to enter their doors. Although the city had suffered many floods, usually only the lowest elevations were affected. Over and over again, veterans of the 1937 Flood reported thinking "It can't happen here." It was generally believed the waters would never exceed the 1884 total of 46.7 feet. City power plants and water pumping stations were designed to withstand a depth of 47 feet, and that was considered safe under any condition. The unprecedented rise in the Ohio River, coupled with water coming up through the sewer system, caught the city unprepared for imminent danger.

On January 21, the flood crest was at 39 feet, already 11 feet above flood stage. Officials announced this threatened to be the third worst flood in the city's history. But on that day Louisville received an additional 3.68 inches of rain, followed by two inches of snow and a driving sleet storm. On this Thursday, the extent of the danger was becoming clear. All roads out of Louisville were blocked except for Shelbyville Road. All rail lines, except the Southern Railway tracks to Knoxville, were water–covered and dangerous. Beargrass Creek swelled out of its banks and blocked Broadway near its eastern terminus. Streetcar service was halted on Broadway, Market, Chestnut, Walnut, Shelby and Portland Avenue. On Parkland's Virginia Avenue, just off Western Parkway, an automobile was submerged to within six inches of its rooftop.

City officials began preparing for a seldom–used contingency. They ordered that the Point, west of the Cut–Off Bridge, be sandbagged with the hope of limiting damage. In the past, sandbag dikes had been built when the possibility of a 42–foot crest was predicted. Only twice before in Louisville's history had the Ohio River reached that height.

Within hours, the roads that had barely been passable by trucks were traversed only by boats. At this time people were still working to remove furniture and other belongings from their homes. Within hours, this would be a luxury they could no longer afford.

Board of Aldermen president Horace A. Taylor, substituting for Mayor Miller who was rapidly returning home from Washington, met with Robert Gregg, superintendent of sewers and Edward S. Schimpler, construction superintendent of the Department of Works. They were joined by Lt. Col. D. O. Elliott of the Army Corps of Engineers and Captain S. J. Horn, his assistant, to plan the sandbag dike.

On Friday, January 22, the city awoke to a dramatic front–page headline in the *Courier–Journal,* "Record Flood May Cut Electricity In City." On that day Louisville received an additional 1.76 inches of rain and the river rose 6.5 feet in 24 hours. The river rose at an unprecedented .3 foot an hour, a figure made even more impressive now that the river was 20

Horace A. Taylor, president of the Board of Aldermen, ran relief efforts while Mayor Neville Miller hurried back from President Roosevelt's inauguration ceremonies in Washington. He was actively engaged in all aspects of the relief effort, often at the front line of rescue work. A hand–written caption on this photo labels Taylor as "The Viking."

1937 Ohio River Flood Photograph Collections (Corwin Short Photos) – 2002.010.017

miles wide at the Falls, rather than its usual one–mile span. Officials of LG&E warned citizens to expect severe limitation in electrical service with a high probability that only essential services like hospitals would receive power generation.

Mayor Miller, now back in Louisville and in command, made the first of his memorable radio addresses to the city. At 11 p.m. he spoke to the population and urged calm. He announced that all city agencies as well as the Red Cross, Volunteers of America, Salvation Army and others were organizing to assist flood victims. *"With the flood liable to go to 47 feet,"* said the Mayor, *"now is the time to think about moving. If your home is below 450 feet above sea level, it will be invaded. If you move early, it can be done with less trouble and more safety."*

Citizens were told to conserve energy and movie houses were closed to save power. The University of Louisville was ordered closed. Shipments of milk were delivered from Chicago because local dairies were out of commission and did not have the electricity to pasteurize. Central Station, one of the city's two railway terminals, located at Seventh Street and River Road, and all approaches were submerged. Union Station on Broadway was still receiving trains, but schedules were haywire with delays, detours and route changes.

Bowman Field, the city's only airport, was deserted as the runways were too wet for heavy planes to land and visibility was very poor. Bus service into the city ceased. The streetcars of the Louisville Railway Company operated on a fraction of their regular routes. Three feet of water over Lexington Road at Payne Street disrupted routes into the safety of the Highlands. The ambitious plan to sandbag River Road in the Point was abandoned as too little and too late.

Immediately upon his arrival in town, Mayor Neville Miller rushed to monitor the rescues taking place in Portland and Shippingport. Contemporary newspaper accounts depict the Mayor, dramatically clad in raincoat and boots, supervising rescues. *(In a wry aside, written in the Mayor's personal scrapbook, now preserved in the University of Louisville Special Collections, Miller adds an editorial correction to this striking image. "NO BOOTS" written in the Mayor's bold hand.)*

His first response to the crisis was characteristic of Neville

The submerged northeast corner of Lexington Road and Grinstead Drive was the site of the Old Kentucky Distillery complex. Part of the grounds was also used as the Louisville Riding Club stable, where riders explored nearby Cherokee Park and the paths following Beargrass Creek. Today one of Louisville Metro's busiest intersections, the site features I–64 on–and–off ramps, and links the Highlands with Crescent Hill.

1937 Ohio River Flood Photograph Collections – 1986.65.05

One of Louisville's two passenger railroad depots, Central Station, was located at Seventh Street and River Road, and was quickly flooded. The other railroad terminus, Union Station on Broadway, continued to operate for a few more days until it also closed. In later years, Central Station served as the original home of Actor's Theatre and Hawley–Cooke Bookstore. The building was destroyed in 1964, during the construction of I–64 through the heart of the city.

Caufield and Shook Collection – 149476

Miller. He called upon local businessmen, civic leaders and officials to assist. He named a stellar flood committee that included William A. Stoll, president, and William E. Morrow, secretary of the Louisville Board of Trade (now Greater Louisville Inc. - the Metro Chamber of Commerce); George Chescheir, city engineer; J. B. Wilson; director of finance; John R. Lindsay and Charles Reiger, Welfare Department; Dunlap Wakefield, director of safety; A. J. Stewart, housing advisor;

Alvin Rosenberg, Frank Hill and T. Kennedy Helm. City government began to operate on a 24–hour schedule.

At this point, relief services moved into high gear. The Rev. John Lowe Fort, secretary of the Louisville Council of Churches announced that 25 churches adjacent to the flooded areas were open to accept refugees. Normal city garbage collection was halted and Allie Rosenberg, head of the Sanitation Department, added 500 extra men to his normal crew of 250, and 300 extra

A woman is carried over the frigid waters by a courteous rescuer. Many people delayed evacuating their homes because of their mistaken belief "it can't happen here." The crest of the Great Flood of 1937 erased all previous flood stages and invaded areas that had previously stayed safe and dry.

R.G. Potter Collection – 176

"...there is really nothing that cannot be done."

L. S. Vance
Chief Engineer
Louisville Water Company

trucks to his normal fleet of 50. Most of these trucks would be used for transporting citizens wishing to leave the rapidly–flooding West End.

The first two city schools were closed. The Robert Fulton and Lower Fulton Schools on River Road were shut, but officials were confident that Shawnee High and Brandeis School could remain open if their basements were continually pumped. Two schools on extreme lower Dixie Highway, Kosmosdale and Medora, were closed due to very high water.

On January 22 the river had passed the historic 1884 high water mark and continued to rise. Citizens were told to go home and stay there.

City police, fire and rescue crews were soon stretched to their absolute limits, with civil servants working around the clock to effect rescues and relief operations. Fire presented one of the greatest dangers during the crisis, especially when water rose too high for fire trucks to reach burning structures. Louisville firemen were reported weeping with frustration because they could not get close enough to fight a fire.

Caufield and Shook Collection – 149497 1/2

But the officials of the city kept their heads nobly. Mayor Neville Miller had done yeoman work mobilizing and augmenting his forces to meet the peril. He took time on the radio to let the people know what was happening. And it is worth recording that, instead of making light of conditions, as officials sometimes mistakenly do, he was completely frank with his townsfolk. He did not pretend that everything looked rosy and that there was no cause for alarm. He told the truth and said, "Prepare to face the worst flood in the history of Louisville, but face it with level heads, and above everything, remain calm!" Then he proceeded to show that, though the inundation probably would be worse than ever before, the city had more resources to cope with it than ever before.

Lowell Thomas,
Hungry Waters

Alvin (Allie) Rosenberg, shown here enjoying a carnival ride, was head of Louisville's Sanitation Department, and provided skilled leadership during the crisis. His department more than doubled in size and helped thousands of refugees escape the West End. Mayor Miller would later recall Rosenberg's canny political wit, when a salesman tried to sell a street–sweeping machine that would replace loyal Democrats. "It can sweep streets all right, but come Election Day, it can't vote," Rosenberg opined.

Herald Post – 4072

Louisville Gas & Electric (LG&E) Company's massive Waterside Plant supplied most of downtown's utility needs. Located near the river at Second and Washington streets, the company's lighted promotional sign proclaimed for decades that Louisville is the "Gateway to the South." On the left is a guard rail of the Louisville Municipal Bridge (today's George Rogers Clark Memorial Bridge), and on the right is the deck of a ferry boat. The house sitting surrounded by water is the second–story of the wharf master's house.

R.G. Potter Collection – 521

LOUISVILLE GAS & ELECTRIC COMPANY

The greatest technical challenges of the Flood were faced by the utility companies that produced Louisville's electricity, gas and drinking water.

The Louisville Gas & Electric Company (LG&E) bore the responsibility for supplying two of those essential needs. As dictated by the technical limitations of that era, all their energy–generating plants were located adjacent to the Ohio River. The massive Waterside Plant located at Second and Washington streets, supplied the bulk of the city's electrical needs. A smaller plant, the Canal Substation, was located on Northwestern Parkway at 20th Street. Both depended upon river barge deliveries of coal to generate electricity.

LG&E's Shippingport Hydroelectric Plant harnessed the power of the Falls of the Ohio. Working with the U.S. Army Corps of Engineers, construction of the massive power plant was completed in 1928. The plant's location caused it to be closed in times of extremely high water. The Hydroelectric Plant had already ceased operation on January 5, weeks before the eventual flood crest.

R.G. Potter Collection – 532

The hydroelectric plant called the Ohio Falls was built in 1927 as a part of the U.S. Army Corps of Engineers' damming of the Falls. This operation, anchored to Shippingport's northern shore, could not generate power when the river level was too high and had temporarily ceased operation on January 5. Despite increasing danger, employees remained on duty in chambers deep under the river's surface to pump out water and maintain bulkheads on the sagging walls.

LG&E operated two gas manufacturing plants, producing a mixture of gas made from coal in these plants and blending it with natural gas. The Beargrass Creek Plant was located north of River Road and west of Zorn Avenue. The Jackson Street plant was at Washington and Jackson streets in Butchertown. Numerous substations, where the gases were mixed and pumped to customers, were located throughout the community. Because so many local industries were forced to cease operations, demand for gas service diminished enough to allow continued service to residences, hospitals and relief stations.

The Flood of 1884 had established the design standards for utility plant construction. Since experts believed the river would never exceed the landmark height of 46.7 feet, modern plants were built to withstand a 47–foot flood stage. Rapidly rising waters during the third week of January ended those optimistic projections.

LG&E president T. Bert Wilson called in all available employees and told them to prepare for possible inundation. Walls of the plants were bulkheaded to increase their stability, pumps began running continuously, and emergency kitchens and sleeping quarters were improvised to accommodate the 400 workers on duty.

The Beargrass Station Gas Plant, operated by LG&E, produced gas from coal and blended it with natural gas to supply homes, businesses and factories with heat. The plant, located north of River Road and west of Zorn Avenue, used barge loads of coal to supply local manufacturing requirements. Because so many factories closed, no curtailment of natural gas service was necessary during the crisis.

Caufield and Shook Collection – 53647

LOUISVILLE WATER COMPANY

Nothing is more fundamental to life than water. In one of the great ironies of the 1937 Flood, more water in the river meant less water in the faucet. On the fourth Friday of January, Louisville's entire drinking water supply depended upon the courage and ingenuity of the 13 workers who manned the Louisville Water Company's Riverside Pumping Station at Zorn Avenue. Water Company president Joseph D. Scholtz supervised an essential public utility with rapidly diminishing resources.

On Saturday, January 23, the Riverside water pumping station was inundated, which drowned the boiler fires, stopping all operations. The Riverside station, with its 1860 Greek Revival pump house and water tower, took water from the adjacent river and pumped it up to the Crescent Hill Reservoir, where it entered huge sedimentation tanks for purification. With the Riverside pumps silent, the city was forced to go on restricted water service. Drinking water was only available for two hours daily, from 8 to 9 a.m., and from 4 to 5 p.m. People were instructed to boil their drinking water and add a drop of iodine to kill germs.

The city's supply of drinking water normally depended upon the 42 million gallons in the Crescent Hill Reservoir and an additional 25 million gallons processed at the recently–built Cardinal Hill Reservoir near Iroquois Park. Without a steady water supply from the river, instead of the normal 67 million gallons available to the city, the two remaining reservoirs could supply only eight million gallons a day for another eight days.

A method of pumping water up to the reservoirs, which were rapidly being depleted, was desperately needed, and an ingenious

The massive machinery of the Louisville Water Company's Riverside Pumping Station was capable of moving thousands of gallons of water up to the Crescent Hill Reservoir, but only when the plant's great boilers were producing steam. Today, the distinctive Greek Revival–style pumping plant and water towers at the end of Zorn Avenue is a National Historic Landmark, but it remains an integral part of Louisville's drinking water supply chain.

1937 Ohio River Flood Photograph Collections – 1982.13.53

river–borne solution was found. The towboat E. T. Slider (commanded by the veteran river man Mr. Slider himself) was secured to the Riverside plant. By using its steam engines, the towboat was able to pump enough flood waters out of the plant to maintain an unsteady supply to the reservoirs.

Water Company Chief Engineer and Superintendent L. S. Vance recorded some of the trials faced by his crews:

On Thursday, January 21st, the telephone communication with the River Station was lost, the wires having been torn down by a floating house. The only communication then, being notes and word of mouth by skiff, which made more or less regular trips to and from the Station with the different station operating crew shifts. Friday morning it became evident that radio would be the only possible means of maintaining the absolutely necessary contact.

Early that Friday morning the Power Company asked us to release them of our electric pump load, they too were having their troubles. We reverted to steam power pumping as soon as possible.

By this time the bulkheads around the pipe openings of the pump house were also leaking but the steam sump pump was able to hold this leakage down. The steam pipes, however, from the boiler house to the pump house were then under flood water. At about 2:30 a.m. that morning, when it became definitely evident that the River Station would go out of operation, the expedient of rationing the remaining water supply to the City was decided upon.

After summarizing the trials faced by his engineers and work crews, L. S. Vance expressed one of the great truths learned by Louisvillians during the Flood: "...*along with other things accomplished by other organizations (the successful response) has proven that there is nothing that really cannot be done.*"

Mayor's Scrapbook – pages 20-B

Mayor's Scrapbook – pages 20-A, 20-B

SOUTHERN BELL TELEPHONE COMPANY AND AT&T

The striking Art Deco–style Southern Bell Telephone Company headquarters on Chestnut Street became a combination dormitory, mess hall, and communications center. When faced with handling the greatest service demand to ever confront a telephone exchange, 400 young Louisville women volunteered to join the regular workforce. When the volunteer operators began their service they did not realize they would remain on duty for 14 consecutive days and nights and live on the seventh, eighth and ninth floors of the office building.

At the first sign of an impending crisis, the company's management shipped gasoline generators and pumps to Louisville to provide power and security. Southern Bell, and its long distance server AT&T, also rushed an additional 450 engineers, linemen and operators to Louisville to keep communications open. Operators facilitated 7,000 long distance calls a day, a 300 percent increase over their normal work load. They accomplished this despite 31,000 telephones being out of order due to breaks in both above and underground cables and wiring.

Acts of sacrifice and originality became the norm for phone personnel. In the Shawnee exchange office, with the building surrounded by water and the basement overflowing, a crew of 14 operators and 20 linemen and mechanics remained on duty, living and working at their jobs. An enterprising young Pleasure Ridge Park operator notified her subscribers that if they wanted to continue their phone service, they would need to donate their automobile batteries. The good people of PRP promptly brought in their batteries to help maintain communications.

The Southern Bell Telephone Company, and its long–distance server AT&T, faced unprecedented demands to carry communications to and from Louisville. Four hundred local women volunteered to serve as operators during the crisis. They, and the company's regular employees, were compelled to stay in the building for two weeks, in dormitories hastily prepared on the upper floors of the city's finest Art Deco–style downtown building.

Caufield and Shook Collection – 126322-0

"He had packed a suitcase with necessities, foreseeing a long stay."

Looking back at her family's experience nearly 70 years after the Flood, Peggy Buckley Bennett remembered the sacrifices made by her father, a telephone executive, and his co–workers:

In January 1937, I was a nine–year–old student at George Rogers Clark Elementary School in Crescent Hill. I lived with my parents, Milton Nicol Buckley and Cecile Payne Buckley, on Galt Avenue mid–way between my school and the relatively new Barret Junior High. There were many children in our neighborhood. The constant rains and threats of flooding had closed the schools much to our delight, as we were totally unaware of what was to follow.

My father was District Traffic Superintendent for AT&T, which meant that he was responsible for the long distance service to thousands of Americans, as Louisville was a switching center for the entire southeast. Eight hundred operators manned the electric powered switchboards in three shifts a day, supported by AT&T engineers and management staffs. It was not unusual for my father to be at his office on holidays such as Christmas and Mothers Day or any holiday when families felt it necessary to touch base; but one Sunday he was to leave and we wouldn't see him for over three weeks.

The Ohio River was above flood stage with waters six feet and more in downtown Louisville. The telephone building shared by AT&T and Southern Bell was and is at Sixth and Chestnut – ten stories of sensitive equipment feeding cables throughout the area. My mother and I drove my father to the Baxter Avenue railroad station where the floodwaters had paused. He had packed a suitcase with necessities, foreseeing a long stay. The county sheriff's department took him down Market Street by boat and I clearly remember watching them go off in the misty rain. Mother and I returned home, safe in Crescent Hill.

The telephone building was now surrounded by water, kept dry by hundreds of sand bags, the switchboards operating on huge generators. The National Guard had brought in canvas cots and blankets and pillows. The operators on duty were isolated and others were called to volunteer to come in and relive them. A large room, which had been the operators' off–duty lounge, was made into a barracks. My father slept in his office, when he was able to snatch a few precious moments of rest.

Fortunately the building housed an adequate cafeteria, as the staffs were there 24 hours–a–day for three weeks. They were able to keep in touch with families by phone, as most central offices out in the city and county maintained some minimal service. Those in downtown and western areas of the city struggled. Service men risked life and limb to string temporary lines and maintain pumps to keep underground cables dry. Police and National Guard troops ferried in food and clean clothing sent by the operators' families.

When the worst was over and some normalcy returned, the faithful telephone people were rewarded with bonuses and extended vacations and the thanks of their community.

Peggy Buckley Bennett

The Water, and the Crisis, Deepens

By Saturday, January 23, the crisis had become acute. All gasoline stations were closed by the Mayor's order to ensure an ample supply for fire, relief and police vehicles. Six thousand Louisvillians were evacuated from their homes and local churches were ordered closed for the next day. An overnight low temperature of ten degrees was predicted and people struggled to locate the small heating devices called Monkey stoves, and the wood or coal to burn in them. Although candles, kerosene lamps and flashlights became difficult to locate, a local store advertised galoshes for 89 cents.

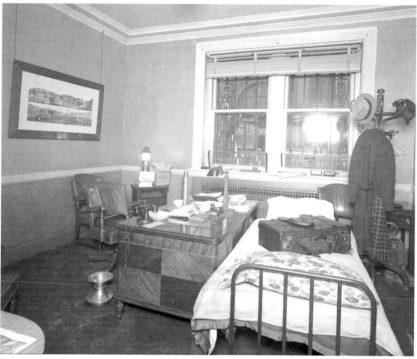

An island of tidiness in a sea of chaos, a banker's office in the First National Bank served an unidentified businessman as a home and office during the crisis. Experienced executives were recruited by the Mayor's Relief Committees to administer emergency relief centers and services. Representatives from every segment of Louisville's community, from chief executives to day laborers, came together to work for the common good.

R.G. Potter Collection – 3468

Downtown buildings were darkened, theaters ordered closed and elevators shut down to conserve electricity. Local banks carried their valuables upstairs and sealed their subterranean vaults. The downtown post office had over $2,000,000 worth of stamped envelopes and postcards in their basement and these were taken to upper floors for safety. All sporting events were cancelled until further notice. One hundred and fifty members of the 138th Field Artillery of the National Guard reported for duty to help protect downtown Louisville.

At the Louisville–Portland Canal, lockmaster E. L. Bankenship moved his staff to the home of Everett Keeling, 2622 Northwestern Parkway. For eight days, Keeling's home became the operational headquarters for the Canal staff.

Across the river, Jeffersonville was ten feet under water and 4,000 people fled the continually rising waters. The flood stage had reached 49.4 feet and police were on patrol to prevent looting from abandoned homes and stores. In Shippingport, only the roofs of the tallest buildings were visible and Towhead Island had completely disappeared.

In the southwestern end of Jefferson County, suffering was particularly intense. Nearly 200 residents of Kosmosdale were loaded on boats supplied by Kosmosdale Portland Cement Company and brought to Louisville. At Medora, numerous houses were sighted floating across Dixie Highway. As houses and buildings drifted downstream, it was reported that thousands of rats had sought sanctuary on floating rooftops in an attempt to avoid drowning.

In Okolona, on Preston Street Road, a mother and her three daughters were rescued while standing shoulder deep in water. Only one family home in the St. Denis Parish on Cane Run Road was not under water. The school and sisters' home, both

located on higher ground, were turned over to refugees, both white and African–American, and a Red Cross clinic established in the rectory. At St. Helen Church, in the heart of the future Shively, the church itself was not affected, but the school's basement was flooded.

St. Paul Church, in Pleasure Ridge Park, remained high and dry on one of the short stretches on Dixie Highway that remained above water. Of the entire 33–mile stretch of Highway 31–W from Louisville to Fort Knox, only three total miles were not flooded. Several families were housed in St. Paul's School, but nearly two–thirds of the parish found shelter at Waverly Hills Sanitarium, a mile–and–a–half to the south, and others at old Kerrick School, a half–mile to the north.

The Standard Oil service station at Third and Brandeis is typical of local stations closed to guarantee enough gasoline for rescue and relief operations. This station, located next to the Confederate Monument near the University of Louisville, offers a gallon of gas for 18 cents. The photo was taken slightly after the Flood's crest, since a high–water oil mark can be seen on the KYSO sign.

Collection of Scott Nussbaum

The Kosmosdale Cement Company, located in the extreme southwestern end of Jefferson County on Dixie Highway, was an early victim of flooding. Over 200 local residents went to the plant and were transported into Louisville by boat. Almost the entire length of Dixie Highway was covered by flood waters.

Postcard Collection – 2000.04.23

Jefferson County, outside the city limits, was home to nearly 3,300 family and commercial farms in 1937. The Crum's Lane area, near Cane Run Road, was especially hard hit by the rising Ohio River. Only one family in the St. Denis Parish was able to remain in its home, with everyone else fleeing the encroaching waters for higher ground.

1937 Ohio River Flood Photograph Collections – 1986.49.11

The original Jewish Hospital, located at 236 East Kentucky, was evacuated when water invaded the basement and closed heating operations. Fifty patients were wrapped in blankets and removed to other medical facilities under the direction of Adeline M. Hughes, superintendent of the hospital. A 22–year old volunteer relief worker, Thomas Snider of Shively, was taken to Sts. Mary and Elizabeth Hospital with frozen feet. Local pharmacies announced that prescriptions endorsed by a physician would be provided free of charge during the duration of the crisis.

In the earliest days of the 1937 Flood, rescues were made using high–riding trucks, many supplied by the Sanitation Department. With waters rising around the clock, boats rapidly became the vehicle of choice. Louisvillians have always enjoyed boating, whether as a trade or for recreation, and learned to know the river. Many local people owned their own boats, knew seamanship and were comfortable on the open waters. They formed the core of the boat crew rescue teams that saved countless lives.

Serving on a rescue boat was exhausting labor, often requiring hours of rowing against violent currents while exposed to cold rain or snow. Several nights the temperatures plummeted into the low teens and three–inch snowfalls were recorded. Heavy woolen clothing was continually soaked and no rest was in sight while the lives of refugees were threatened. One veteran Coast Guardsman gave his assessment of conditions, *"I served three years in Alaska waters, but never felt water as cold as this. You can even hear the frogs' teeth chatter when they try to croak."*

Piloting a boat through the flood–covered streets meant running a gauntlet of submerged fences, cars or debris. Many boats bottomed out or snagged their outboard motors on downed wires and other flotsam. They maneuvered through turbulent eddies in snow and hailstorms. Half of their time was spent making rescues at night, since emergencies would not wait until morning.

A Portland neighborhood legend is the tale of a policeman with superhuman strength rescuing the Sisters of Charity and the Blessed Sacrament. The Sisters maintained the small St.

"I went through hell and high water today."

Brainard Platt
Courier–Journal reporter
January 24, 1937

RISING WATERS – SOARING SPIRITS

"This means more to me than my life."

Sister Theresa, SCN

Railroad container cars floated in the L&N yard at First and Main streets. The buoyant cars drifted into buildings and were hazards, until local officials began filling the containers with river water to weigh them down. This scene is two blocks west of today's Slugger Field.
Goodman–Paxton – Box 30 Item 4799

Ann's Convent at 24th and Portland Avenue to provide a home for teachers in West End parochial schools. With waters rapidly encroaching, they called for help. Their task was to transport to safety the sacramental Sacred Vessels used to celebrate Mass, a duty that technically requires a priest rather than a nun. By telephone, they were instructed to wrap the vessels and place them in a leather case and take them to the nearest church.

Sister Theresa, the Sacristan, clutched the suitcase carrying her precious load while she, and seven Sisters of Charity, joined a two–man crew in a rescue boat. After bouts of trouble with a faulty motor, the boat finally started up and roared into a telephone pole, splitting the boat in half. Submerged in the swollen stream that was Portland Avenue, faithful Sister Theresa retained her grip on the suitcase which she would not surrender. A policeman in a rescue boat rushed to the sinking sister and told her to drop her bag, and she replied, *"This means more to me than my life."* Already in a state of near exhaustion, the officer reported that as soon as he touched the sister he felt a supernatural strength allowing him to lift the drenched nun, and the suitcase, into the rescue boat and eventual safety.

Rescue boatmen were the front–line troops of flood rescue. In their rare moments of rest, they were not even allowed to smoke due to the danger from floating gasoline or oil slicks. Some of their biggest problems came from dealing with those they were rescuing. Many refused to leave their second–story apartments and were panic–stricken. Others tried to carry away more than reasonably could be transported. Pet owners struggled to save their dogs, cats and canarybirds. The rescue workers welcomed all aboard their boats.

THIS BOAT OR MOTOR WAS USED FOR LIFE SAVING IN THE LOUISVILLE FLOOD – 1937 – NEVILLE MILLER, MAYOR

Mayor's Scrapbook

Mrs. Helen Fischer (holding on to porch), a friend and her faithful Chow dog were rescued from their home at Floyd and Breckinridge streets by two boatmen. The rapidly rising waters made it impossible to carry away possessions, but pets were routinely saved and taken to relief stations. On the left of photo is the old Male High School football field.

R.G. Potter Collection – 513

At the 32nd and Broadway relief station, the rate of rescue was 75 persons an hour. Relief stations at the Shawnee Park Police Station, 27th and Broadway, and at 44th and Market constantly shuttled boats to and from rapidly flooding homes and businesses. When Coast Guard reinforcements began arriving, their professionalism and training provided a welcome rest for volunteer crews. One hundred eighty Coast Guard boats were shipped to Louisville by railways to supply large strong vessels capable of besting the surging waters.

ATTENTION, RESCUE WORKERS!

Rescue workers and persons in rowboats in zones affected by flood waters are urged to watch for a fleet of sound trucks, bearing special instructions from relief headquarters as to rescue measures and emergency bulletins. These trucks, patrolling as near as possible to flooded areas, carry radio receivers tuned to WHAS, radiophone of the *Courier–Journal* and *The Louisville Times*. The facilities of this station have been turned over to authorities in charge of rescue work.

The amplifiers of the trucks may be heard for a mile and should speed rescue parties to marooned families. All persons in urgent need of help are asked to try to communicate with the station.

Courier–Journal
January 24, 1937

The O.K. Storage Building, located where Barret meets Broadway, was the busiest of all rescue stations, landing an average of 200 refugees an hour. From this location, the rescued moved up the elevated section of Broadway toward Baxter Avenue and safety.

Caufield and Shook Collection – 149499

The Legendary B–13 and its Sea–Going Pastor

Rescue stations were temporary locations, placed nearest to the water's edge to dispatch or receive boats. Each station was mobile to stay ahead of the rising waters, and each received alphabetical and numerical designations. The most celebrated of all the relief station boat crews was B–13, located at the O.K. Storage Warehouse at Broadway and Barret. This landing site started refugees on their path to Baxter Avenue and safety. During the peak of the Flood, the boat crews of B–13 made more rescues than any other station, with 200 refugees landing every hour. Four hundred power boats operated by 700 volunteers made routine excursions to the island that was downtown Louisville.

B–13 was a station so well organized that the crew distilled their own water; created their own repair shops; made spotlights out of coffee cans and generated their own lights.

The B–13 crew was a fortuitous mixture of personalities with diverse abilities and generous spirits. Volunteers from Massachusetts – skilled deep–sea fishermen – arrived in Louisville with one of their distinctive boats, a Gloucester dory. When their volunteer service was completed, they left the dory in Louisville and donated it to the local Sea Scouts.

The Barret and Broadway station was commanded by one of the truly charismatic personalities of the Great Flood. Reverend Dr. Homer C. "Doc" Lindsay, pastor of the First Lutheran Church, commanded with the swagger and confidence of General George Patton. Described as "the dynamic hip–booted raincoated Doc", the good reverend was not a stranger to water. He held a pilot's license on the Great Lakes and a first mate's license on ocean–going ships. After the Great Flood, he was awarded an honorary pilot's license for a Broadway motor boat.

The camaraderie and friendships established during the glory days of B–13 were not allowed to fade away. One year after the '37 Flood, the group assembled again at the O.K. Storage Warehouse and went across the street to the Concordia Lutheran Church for sandwiches and steaming cups of coffee. This familiar relief station fare was served under the supervision of Reverend C. Eberhard, just as it had been during the Flood. To further enhance the nostalgic reunion, two outboard motors were kept running, and simulated "Send a Boat" messages were broadcast by loudspeaker.

To paraphrase Mark Twain's description of riverboat pilots, "Their pride was the pride of kings," and the B–13 crew voted to organize themselves into an alumni association and meet yearly. The members of the general B–13 staff, who served under Dr. Lindsay, included L. F. Kennett, Ted Zenishek, E. F. DeVol, C.E. Vinson, Verne L. Lovett, Dr. Carl J. Johnson, Reverend Dr. C. A. Eberhard and Edward Q. Showers.

Among the alumni who were asked to keep their flood positions were Dr. G. P. Beutel, in charge of hospitalization; H. Nelson

O.K. Storage was the headquarters of Rescue Station B–13, the largest and most successful of all relief centers. Over 700 volunteers manned 400 boats of every description to transport people from the island that was the downtown business district of Louisville.

1937 Ohio River Flood Photograph Collections – 1986.45.24

The volunteers of Rescue Station B–13 developed a rare camaraderie, and maintained a kind of alumni association after the Flood. The group, made up of a remarkable collection of boatmen, mechanics, business executives and ministers, were known for their indomitable spirit and resourcefulness.

R.G. Potter Collection – 3436

DeVol, storekeeper; Robert Gibson, property and purchases; J. H. Rose, Charles G. Klapheke and W. F. Scoggins, boat dispatchers; Fred Abrams and James Abrams, boat hull repairing; Frank Fichterkessing, Fehr Kellner, Fred Gerlach and Jimmy Butler, radio and electrical engineering; J. C. Bennett, Roy Akin, Joe Schadt, mechanical repairing; Charles J. Weber and William Abell, examining staff; Arthur Unglaub, traffic; Robert Martin and Robert Ritchie, dispatching office; J H. Welford, sanitary engineering; E. G. Luening and I. J. Martin, housing and distribution of food.

Members of the advisory committee included Joseph D. Scholtz, Mark Ethridge, Col. Henry J. Stites, Col. A. W. Lissauer, Col. A. T. McCormack, Dr. Hugh Leavell, Sam H. McMeekin, Dr. J. D. Trawick and Roy W. Burks.

B–13 was commanded by the Reverend Homer C. "Doc" Lindsay, pastor of the First Lutheran Church on Broadway from 1933 until 1942. Prior to becoming a minister, Reverend Lindsay held a pilot's license for the Great Lakes and a first mate's license for ocean–going ships. "Doc" Lindsay is shown here (top center in black overcoat) leading a prayer for the boatmen, soldiers and policemen who formed his unusual command.

1937 Ohio River Flood Photograph Collections – 1986.45.23

An Act of Singular Bravery

Not all rescues were performed in boats. The most celebrated rescue involved both remarkable bravery and the city's worst drowning accident. A Louisville police officer, Lawrence W. Claycomb, and Army private Robert T. Mueller, drowned when their combat car skidded down Peterson Avenue's steep brick pavement and plunged into 15 feet of water. Two other passengers in the armored vehicle were saved through the courageous actions of a local banker and a telephone repairman.

F. J. Von Hoven, an employee of Liberty National Bank and Trust Company, was following behind the mechanized combat car as it descended Peterson toward Grinstead Drive. When the armored car, complete with machine gun and small cannon, blew a tire and lost control, the vehicle skidded down the slick street and plunged into 15 feet of water. Von Hoven stopped and directed his headlights into the bubbling water. He ran to the water's edge and grabbed Fort Knox soldier Hoy Davis by the hair, pulling him to safety.

A young telephone lineman, Robert Lee Meyer, witnessed the event while installing phone service to the emergency hospital being set up in Barret Junior High. Climbing down the pole and leaping into the frigid water, Meyer swam 30 feet to the wreck and took hold of Private Harold Harrington. After pulling the soldier to safety, Meyer swam back to the vehicle in a vain attempt to save the remaining passengers. Despite his heroic rescue attempt he was unable to enter the turret of the combat car to reach the two doomed passengers.

A year after the Flood, Meyer's heroism was recognized by Southern Bell Telephone and Telegraph Company and he was presented the Theodore N. Vail Award, the firm's highest national recognition for community service. Typically laconic and self–effacing, young Robert Lee Meyer responded when receiving the award, *"I don't feel that any special credit is due me. Any member of the organization would have done the same thing."*

A Dry Blanket and a Cup of Hot Coffee...

The quick organization of boat rescue stations indicated that the extent of the flooding was unprecedented. Local authorities, under the direction of Mayor Neville Miller, conducted all relief activities. Volunteer committees were set up to assist in evacuation, feeding, housing, and to help boost morale. With the extent of the disaster becoming obvious, city officials began to move relief stations further away from the immediate flood area. They now realized that far greater suffering, and additional water heights, faced every proposed relief operation.

John Richardson, Director of Welfare, and Dr. E. C. Blom

selected fire stations to serve as initial emergency centers. Stations at 16th and Main, Eighth and Hill, Hancock and Jefferson, Logan and St. Catherine and Fourth and K streets were pressed into service. Emergency canteens were established to provide food and warmth to those just being taken off rescue vessels. Canteens were manned at 1860 Frankfort Avenue at the Third Lutheran Church; 1368 Payne at the City Workhouse; at the downtown Neighborhood House; and Walnut Street Baptist Church at Third and St. Catherine.

Additional food stations were opened at Sacred Heart School, 27th and Broadway; Goodwill Industries, Eighth

Refugees arriving at a relief station maintained in the Louisville Hotel were able to make telephone calls, file missing person reports and warm their feet. After being processed by Red Cross or WPA workers, the refugees were transported to more permanent locations in the Highlands or shipped out of town by rail.

Caufield and Shook Collection – 149593

and Market; and Brown & Williamson Tobacco Company, 12th and Hill. The *Courier–Journal* reported that a center *"was opened at 912 W. Chestnut for Negroes, although Negroes will not be refused meals at the other locations."*

The Board of Education opened 44 schools that were out of reach of the water. Shelters were also opened at the Crescent Hill Methodist Church and at the Snead Manufacturing Building (today's Glassworks) on West Market. Downtown's Herman Straus Building was used as a general collection and storage base.

With the new shelters up and operating, the next great challenge was to get people out of the dangerous and deteriorating flooded areas and into places of safety. The rescue stage of the operation would prove to be the most compelling chapter of the Great Flood story.

Workers supplied by the WPA prepared tens of thousands of hot meals for refugees. This station, located on the fifth floor of the Snead Building (today's Glassworks) prepared food supplied by the Red Cross. During the height of the crisis in Louisville and Southern Indiana, the American Red Cross was feeding 230,000 flood victims a day.

1937 Ohio River Flood Photograph Collections – 2001.041.2

Worry is evident on the faces of two refugees registering at a missing person bureau at the Highland Branch Library. The Louisville Free Public Library system, with its branch offices located in many neighborhoods, was a primary source for humanitarian aid for thousands. Coordinating the growing lists of missing persons required the attention of thousands of volunteers and WPA workers.

Louisville Free Public Library Collection – 1992.18.028

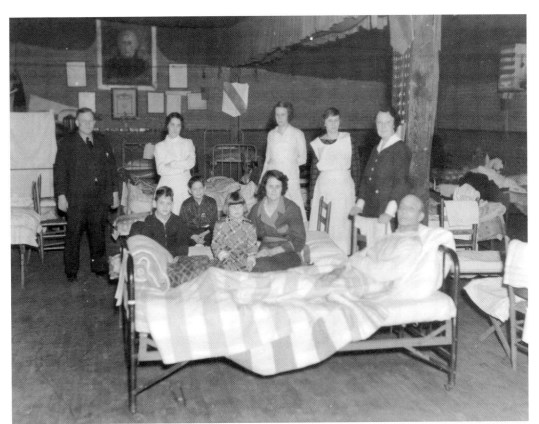

The Snead Building, located at Ninth and Market streets, was the first stop for people fleeing the West End. Some remained throughout the '37 Flood, but many others were transported to the Jefferson County Armory (now Louisville Gardens) for processing and humanitarian services. Officials estimated that over 75,000 individuals were served in the Armory building during the Flood.

1937 Ohio River Flood Photograph Collections – 2001.041.33

"Send a boat."

People's most pressing need was for accurate information, and efficient communication became a high local priority. Louisville's 1937 Flood provided one of the great chapters in the history of American broadcast journalism, and WHAS Radio deserves the credit. To any veteran of the Flood, the most familiar phrase was WHAS' famous call, "SEND A BOAT." This familiar phrase became the slogan and motto of the Great Flood as emergency relief was directed to critical areas over the public airways. WHAS Radio stayed on the air for 187 continuous hours broadcasting its messages of public service.

WHAS was the central source of public information. During the crisis they received and transmitted over 16,500 messages helping to direct rescue boats to danger areas, locate missing persons, instruct utility workers on procedures and calm the unsettled population. The station, under the direction of station manager Credo Harris, dispatched five field crews consisting of an announcer and an engineer, to broadcast warnings and news. One team was stationed on the 19th floor of the Kentucky Home Life Building, Fifth and Jefferson, and used binoculars to describe the river's turbulent passage.

Two of the most recognizable heroes of the '37 Flood were WHAS announcers Pete Monroe and Foster Brooks (shown on opposite page), who were equipped with portable equipment and ranged the area providing vitally important news. At the beginning of the flood, West End resident Foster Brooks was being paid $20 a week as a station–break announcer. Working with the station's chief announcer, Pete Monroe, the pair put themselves at the scene of danger and both gained national acclaim for their insightful reporting. Far greater fame would come decades later for Foster Brooks, when working as a comedian, he perfected his "Lovable Lush" character and starred on television shows and in nightclub reviews. Following the Flood, WHAS employees – Foster Brooks included – received a $25 bonus and time off to catch up on sleep. Afterwards, Brooks returned to his job announcing station breaks.

After electrical outages shut down most home radios, people listened on their car radios or crystal sets, as few radios were battery–powered at this time. Because WHAS Radio's signal was a clear–channel 50,000 watts, most of the eastern seaboard of the United States could listen to the flood broadcasts. These broadcasts electrified America and the nation rallied to send supplies and assistance to suffering Louisville. Broadcast journalism, then still in its pioneer days, has rarely risen to the standards of excellence exhibited by WHAS during the 1937 Flood crisis.

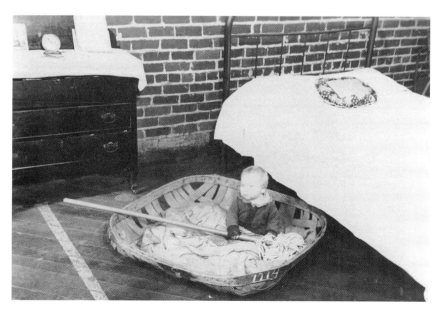

A traditional tobacco basket is pressed into service as a baby's playpen, and a mop becomes a toy in a warehouse relief center. Improvisation and creativity were hallmarks of Louisvillians during the '37 Flood. When normal procedures became impossible, people used their common sense and found another way.

Goodman–Paxton – Box 30 Item 4824

Rabbi Solomon Bazell, of Temple B'rith Sholom, made minor broadcast history on a WHAS radio program. His temple, located at Second and College streets, was surrounded by water and inaccessible to his congregation.

Herald Post – 1254

The Rabbi, Dizzy and Paul

Rabbi Solomon Bazell made one of the most memorable addresses ever broadcast by WHAS radio, before or after the Flood. What he said is not remembered, but his costume bordered on the surreal. Rabbi Bazell and his friend J. S. Reich had been volunteering in the Highlands relief effort when it came time to head downtown for his scheduled radio appearance. On the way to present his sermon, the Rabbi's boat overturned near the Pontoon Bridge and both men were soaked.

Rabbi Bazell was to appear on the radio, rather than his regular service because B'rith Sholom Temple, Second and College streets, was surrounded by flood waters. When the Rabbi arrived, just moments before his broadcast, the staff of WHAS took away his pants to dry, gave him a blanket to wrap himself in, and provided a sweatshirt. The rabbi gave his sermon standing at the microphone with no pants and a sweatshirt bearing a photo of baseball stars Paul and Dizzy Dean. The slogan on the sweatshirt read "Me and Paul."

Mayor's Scrapbook – Page 76

"Louisville's flood has been the means of demonstrating the underlying power of the people. Unorganized but able, inexperienced for the most part but willing, thousands of citizens responded to the call and by their almost superhuman efforts transported to safety, within a space of three days, 230,000 persons, whose homes had been engulfed by the swirling waters."

Courier–Journal Editorial

R.G. Potter Collection– 537

"...rehabilitation, the greatest task of all."

Courier–Journal
January 28, 1937

An editorial, "Louisville Carries On," appeared in the *Courier–Journal* of January 28, and commented on the central role played by WHAS and the state of crisis and recovery.

While the Salvation Army has a great tradition of going directly to a crisis, rarely does the crisis come to its own doorstep. The Salvation Army Industrial Home for Men, located at 330 E. Chestnut, received persons in need at their front door and provided relief to thousands.

1937 Ohio River Flood Photograph Collections – 1979.47.5

Now that the Ohio's raging waters have come to a stand and flood–beleaguered residents have been removed to a place of safety, it becomes possible to collect one's thoughts and to pause for a moment to appraise the remarkable work of rescue and relief which one–third of Louisville has done for the other two–thirds.

But, lest the mistaken impression be created that the work of succor is at an end, it should immediately be added that it has only begun. Active direct relief must go on for at least two weeks before rehabilitation, the great task of all, begins. To complete this monumental task, to restore what has been destroyed, is the work of months–and for this task Louisville will welcome the material aid of its neighbors and the Nation.

Louisville's flood has been the means of demonstrating the underlying power of the people. Unorganized but able, inexperienced for the most part but willing, thousands of citizens responded to the call and by their almost superhuman efforts transported to safety, within a space of three days, 230,000 persons, whose homes had been engulfed by the swirling waters.

This could not have been possible without the radio. Indeed, the catastrophe was radio's opportunity – and it has proved radio's triumph.

Radio was the voice of authority. It was the directing commanding general of the flooded area. It issued the impersonal orders, and thousands of workers in flatboats and skiff, power boat, steamboat, and surfboat, automobile, truck and tractor listened and obeyed.

But with all its power, all its authority, all the night and day efforts of the men who worked in relays at the microphone, the radio would have been helpless without the information, the appeals for aid, the news, the orders from police, military, and civil authority which came over the telephone.

And each depended, in turn, upon auxiliary power plants which kept the service going.

Thus even the mechanical forces which helped to overcome the flood's work proved co–operation was necessary, that co–operation which, transformed into human activity, accomplished a task of feeding, clothing and housing refugees in a manner probably never approached for speed and thoroughness in any other major disaster, even in wartime.

The manner in which Louisville's neighbors, the cities and towns to the east untouched by flood, responded to the emergency was an exemplification of honest Kentucky hospitality and true Christianity. And no lines of color

or creed were drawn anywhere. The brotherhood of man was proved by works, not words.

No single individual can be credited with being the directing brain of all this vast co–operative endeavor, but certainly a word of gratitude must be spoken for the energizing effort of Mayor Neville Miller who headed the work of rescue from his post at City Hall, which he has not left throughout the entire emergency period. His calmness has been inspiration to his colleagues, his cheerfulness a tonic, his ability to see through a situation, to analyze it, and to find a solution the greatest single asset to successful accomplishment of an enormous effort.

Louisville, despite the blow, carries on. If its neighbors will continue to send food, fuel and supplies, it can continue to care for the refugees until the waters subside. Then, as rehabilitation begins, the Nation must help, as it has always helped in such major catastrophes.

Co–operative human endeavor has met and will triumph over the disaster wrought by the flood. Next the matter of adequate preventive work must be taken up – and pushed to a solution. Flood can be controlled. The horrors of 1937 must not be repeated.

THE VENICE OF LOUISVILLE   LOU, KY.
#5   FOURTH & ORMSBY   2-9-37

Extraordinary scenes became commonplace during the '37 Flood. In a photo entitled "The Venice of Louisville," onlookers watch a raft cross Fourth Street near Ormsby and the Puritan Apartments. Taken on February 9, 1937, the Ohio River had already been above flood stage since January 15.

Royal Photo Studio Collection – 50304

Louisville's Bingham family owned and operated both WHAS and the *Courier–Journal* and *Times* (the morning and afternoon newspapers published jointly during the crisis). Patriarch Robert Worth Bingham was in England, serving as America's Ambassador to the Court of St. James. He continually monitored conditions in Louisville and rushed home as quickly as possible.

His son Barry Bingham, Sr. directed the family's media companies to use every effort to serve the public good. Even at the peak of the crisis, Bingham standards of excellence were maintained. When power to run the giant presses was no longer available, a skeleton staff of reporters, photographers and editors worked by lantern light to produce the barest outline of a daily newspaper, the Flood Editions. Limited press runs of the Flood Editions were printed in Shelbyville on January 25 and 26 and in the *Lexington Leader's* plant until February 5. Malcolm Bayley, of the *Courier–Journal's* editorial board, explained the rationale behind their publication:

"We are printing an abbreviated paper and sending it to Louisville and other towns in the flood-stricken area at the direction of Barry Bingham, our publisher, principally in order to combat the terrible rumors prevalent in Louisville concerning the situation there," the speaker said. In referring to rumors that countless numbers of bodies were floating down flooded streets in Louisville and that numbers of persons have been burned to death "like rats" in buildings surrounded by water, Mr. Bayley said all this was untrue.

"Every one is a lie," he added.

He also branded as untrue rumors that disease and pestilence had set in on the flood-stricken area of Louisville.

"We are attempting to circulate paper in the Highlands and other 'high and dry' sections there in order to put to rest all these disquieting rumors and ease the worries of the people of Louisville."

Courier-Journal
January 29, 1937

Judge Robert Worth Bingham, Ambassador to Great Britain, hurried back to Louisville with his wife Aleen as soon as the extent of the crisis became clear. Newspapers in London contacted the *Courier–Journal* to inquire if the Ambassador's Crestwood home was in any danger of flooding. Local reporters were happy to report that Mr. Bingham's home was in no danger.

Herlad Post – 1297

Even when they lacked the electrical power needed to run their great presses, the *Courier–Journal* and *Louisville Times* never missed a day of publication. Very limited numbers of Flood Edition specials were produced at newspaper plants in Shelbyville and Lexington to provide news for an information–starved population. The newspaper's purposes in publishing these special editions were to curtail rumors and calm the public's nerves.

A small coterie of reporters, editors and photographers worked around–the–clock in impossible conditions to assemble their daily newspaper. Kerosene lamps provided illumination, and reporters donned hip–boots to gather the news. The copy desk was manned by Glenn Kendall, Herman Landau, Malcolm Bayley and J. N. Bacon, Jr. At one point in their journalistic endeavors, the staff published a small notice asking that someone send them cigarettes.

Courier-Journal and Louisville Times

"Jeffersonville now entirely under water."

No community suffered greater disruption than Jeffersonville, Indiana. The entire downtown business center was submerged, and most buildings had water to the second–floor windows. Over 3,800 of the 3,900 houses in the town were flooded.

Goodman-Paxton – Box 6 Item 303

The flood struck both the Indiana and Kentucky shores with devastating impact. On January 22, the levee in Jeffersonville failed and water poured into the city. Falling Run and Silver Creek surged out of their banks and areas in New Albany that had always been considered high and dry were invaded. The same relief forces that aided Louisville – the WPA, Red Cross and Civilian Conservation Corps – found additional demand for their services in Indiana.

All highways out of the towns were blocked except for Silver Street leading to Charlestown Road. As in Louisville, water service was reduced to two hours daily and utilities struggled to maintain even minimal service. Officials estimated that at its peak, the volume of the Ohio River sent nearly a billion gallons of water a second past New Albany's shore.

Of New Albany's 6,617 residential structures, 3,515 were affected. Forty–eight industrial plants, 319 commercial properties, 11 school buildings and 21 churches were in the flooded area. Necessity was still the mother of invention, and New Albany's Fire Department came up with the original idea of building a huge raft of oil barrels and telephone poles. On the raft they placed a fire engine pumper, and the entire floating fire station was towed to fires in the town.

A small island emerged at the northern end of Louisville's Municipal (Second Street) Bridge and over 300 refugees lived out the flood in the Colgate Palmolive Plant. A cow and two pigs wandered onto the artificial island and provided fresh meat for several days. Holy Trinity Catholic Church was converted into a commissary to feed the 300 WPA workers engaged in relief help.

Despite all, people were able to maintain a positive attitude and even a sense of humor. One local lady had extended invitations for a luncheon B.F. (before the flood). With the inevitable cancellation of the event, the lady followed up by issuing "flood checks" to her guests.

Love overcomes all obstacles, even a cataclysmic flood. For a young New Albany man, Harold Penninger, 21, it was love at first sight when he met 16–year–old Kathryn Belles. They met in a relief station when Harold was singing and playing his guitar, and they were married on March 11. The happy young couple spent their honeymoon in a New Albany refugee camp.

Fire Department Ready for All
Emergencies
New Albany, Ind., 1937 Flood ©

New Albany Fire Department officials came up with an ingenious way to transport fire–fighting equipment to conflagrations. A large floating raft of oil drums and poles was constructed, and a pumper engine loaded on to the vessel. During a fire, the unique floating fire engine could be towed to where it was needed.

Postcard Collection – 1990.19.7

A Hoosier Log

No community endured greater devastation during the '37 Flood than Jeffersonville, Indiana. Of the 3,900 homes in the town, 3,800 were inundated. Virtually the entire population of 15,000 was evacuated. Through excerpts from the telephone log book of the Indiana National Guard, a minute–by–minute account of the crisis emerges. The official communications impart a sense of emergency that needs little explanation.

The log book chronicles the trials of governmental red tape, failing communications, a deteriorating transportation system and foul weather. The log book provides a dramatic running account, as the threat to the Indiana Falls Cities grows during four frightful days in January 1937.

At Intersection of Silver and Spring Sts.
New Albany, Ind., 1937 Flood

Boatmen were forced to steer their vessel beneath the overhead traffic signal at the intersection of Silver and Spring streets in New Albany. The community was isolated from Jeffersonville and Louisville when high water closed bridges over creeks and the Ohio River.

Postcard Collection – 1990.19.11

The Colgate Palmolive plant, at the north end of the Second Street Municipal Bridge, became an island home for over 300 refugees. The large industrial complex, originally a state prison, provided ample space, but supplying food and materials by boat proved to be a challenge for Red Cross and Indiana National Guardsmen.

Postcard Collection – 1990.18.8

Thursday, January 21, 1937

A.M. – Authority granted to Captain Henry Fleischer, New Albany, to call out 50 men and 3 officers for Guard duty.

P.M. – Alldredge at Mt. Vernon and Fleischer at New Albany have been authorized to feed their men at restaurants for an amount not to exceed 40¢ each.

1:57 P.M. – Called Captain Fleischer and authorized him to release any National Guard property needed in the emergency to the representatives of the American Red Cross.

8:30 P.M. - Mr. Hughes, of the Board of Public Works, Jeffersonville, Indiana, called for the Mayor of Jeffersonville and stated that they will have to take care of 4500 people. Six or seven feet of water will be in the town this afternoon. It is coming one foot over the levee and the town will be badly flooded by early afternoon.

8:45 P.M. - Alldredge, Mt. Vernon, reports that the situation there is very bad, that it will be necessary for them to evacuate 200 to 300 families and that they will be in need of several tents and stoves. These stoves were ordered through Fort Harrison yesterday afternoon but to the present time have not been received. We are calling Ft. Harrison in regard to this order for tents and stoves. Alldredge reports that it is getting very cold and it is sleeting and raining in Mt. Vernon.

9:15 P.M. - Captain Fleischer, New Albany, still in need of 500 cots and 2000 blankets. Jeffersonville has three school buildings and one warehouse for housing. No looting at the present time. 2 Officers and 45 men out. Authority granted to put on more men.

Friday, January 22, 1937

12:10 P.M. - Captain Fleischer called. States that half of Jeffersonville is isolated. It is the estimate by Army officials that 4,000 people will be housed in the Quartermaster Depot before night. Lights will be on until water raises five to six feet more but water okay. Mr. Good, Chairman of the American Red Cross, states that there are at least 1000 marooned in the isolated section of Jeffersonville. It is estimated that one-half have their own bedding. Request 1,000 cots and 2,000 blankets for this isolated section. It will be necessary to go through New Albany into Louisville and back over the Municipal Bridge, as this section is adjacent to this bridge.

1:15 P.M. - No telephone communication in Jeffersonville. Water stands 6' in Main St. Expect lights to go out in 2 or 3 hours. Raining. Red Cross representative out on tug so cannot contact. Wants all lanterns available - and kerosene.

3:15 P.M. - Captain Fleischer at Jeffersonville called. Wants to confiscate boats in warehouse. Owner unknown. Recommend having the Mayor or Red Cross do this. Keep National Guard out. Want power boats. Current too swift for row boats.

6:45 P.M. - Report from his officer at Jeffersonville is that the Quartermaster Depot has been opened and they have taken care of the refugees there. There is a Coast Guard boat there and they think that the boat is taking care of the isolated districts which they haven't been able to reach and take supplies to. This officer is to keep in touch with ft. Harrison.

11:00 P.M. - Following wire sent to Secretary of War - "State of Indiana has granted authority to the State of Kentucky to use all tentage and cots stored at Fort Knox, Kentucky to be used in flood relief - signed - Straub"

Saturday, January 23, 1937

1:00 A.M. - Serum has been placed on Ft. Harrison convoy for Jeffersonville.

1:40 A.M. - Captain Fleischer called from Louisville Police Dept. Is going back to Jeffersonville and then New Albany later. The bridge is open from New Albany to Louisville. Water is rising. There is from 2 - to 3 inches of snow. Temperature 16 degrees. Jeffersonville cut in two by water. 4000 people in the Quartermaster Depot.

9:50 A.M. - Called C. Wilson, WPA and was notified that they have in transit ten (10) trucks of food for Jeffersonville. It is thought that it would probably be necessary to send this convoy either to Seymour or Speed, Indiana, and make transfer to Pennsylvania R.R. in order to deliver same to Jeffersonville.

10:03 A.M. - Capt. Fleischer called from New Albany and reported he was in Jeffersonville about one and one half hours ago. 500 to 600 white and colored (mixed) people in school house. Capt. Cornwall trying to segregate them. No looting or trouble of any kind. All the boats are hauling people and food only. Colgate Factory - 350 people there, necessary to contact them via boat. Another school house isolated, 50 people there who must be supplied with food. Boats are being utilized for this purpose only. Boats rowed by hand. No spare boats available for any purpose other than for delivery of food and supplies to isolated districts. Although no looting has taken place up to now, indications point to looting as soon as the water recedes, which will undoubtedly necessitate a call for armed troops.

Government Depot available, and is capable of taking care of people brought to them. Necessary to row the food across the south side. Train load of food arrived at the Government Depot yesterday. As soon as they get all the people taken care of in the marooned area, they are going to try to get the people away from the Municipal Bridge.

Water is hitting at the east end of New Albany now, and is within one and one-half blocks of the Armory. If it gets to the Armory, will have to move people; however, water must raise 2 feet. Convoy of serum isn't in yet. Serum to be turned over to Dr. Adair - can't find him.

Captain Fleischer is retiring for rest, and has placed Capt. Proctor in charge of New Albany, and Capt. Cornwall in charge at Jeffersonville. He has directed them to make their reports direct to this office.

11:30 A.M. - Judge Bradshaw, District Commissioner of the American Legion, called and volunteered the services of the Legion for any purpose we may need them.

2:45 P.M. - Call from Capt. Fleischer at New Albany. States that the 1700 blankets arrived. The serum and blankets have arrived at Jeffersonville. There has been some looting at the pond on the other side of Jeffersonville. New Albany has plenty of room for the ones who are evacuating now. Taking care of the furniture. The housing situation is worse in Jeffersonville. About 500 to 600 in the schoolhouse. Putting them all in the Quartermaster Depot now instead of the school.

9:25 P.M. - Capt. Fleischer called from New Albany and stated that he thought that he had made his last trip from Jeffersonville. Due to water rising he could not make another one. In a very short time Jeffersonville will be isolated from New Albany….The Red Cross is doing exceptionally good work in Jeffersonville and are feeding 3,500 refugees daily. The WPA. is doing the best work in New Albany. The Red Cross is not doing so well there as there are too many "big shots" trying to run it. At least thirty power boats are needed in New Albany and Jeffersonville. In fact they can use all the power boats they can get.

Sunday, January 24, 1937

12:40 A.M. - Mr. Evans of Sears and Roebuck called and said that they are ready to dispatch the following: Rockport 10 boats and 10 motors; New Albany - 6 boats with motors and 22 boats without motors; Jeffersonville - 12 boats and 12 motors. They are ready to leave now by Company transportation.

2:30 A.M. - We have received at this time 378 pair hip boots.

3:20 A.M. - Call from Jeffersonville. The situation is getting worse. It is raining hard in New Albany at this time. It will be more difficult now to get boats from New Albany to Jeffersonville. Half of the west end of New Albany is under water. It is impossible to get into Kentucky on the K & I bridge. The approaches on the Kentucky side are under water. The entire 128th F.A. (Field Artillery) is out in Louisville.

4:50 A. M. - From Red Cross at Aurora (telephone) Water tanks needed badly. Milk can needed for the distribution of water. There is a good supply of milk but they need paper containers in order to distribute this. They need kerosene and kerosene cans. They are getting fuel. Probably will need cots and blankets. It s raining hard at this time. Soup kitchen being operated by C. C. C.

5:40 A. M. - Capt. Fleischer called, and this is the latest information available from Jeffersonville, and has been received from two people who got out of Jeffersonville over the Pennsylvania Railroad and worked their way over the K & I into New Albany. The water at the present time is just outside of the Government Depot. Two feet more and the water will be into the Depot. The people will be safe for five more feet. There are about four or five thousand people in the Depot. They are having great difficulty in getting the people to evacuate their homes now, which will make it necessary to remove them by boats later today. The situation is very bad. The boats have not arrived at this time. Due to the difficulty they are having in removing these people, the officials of New Albany are considering the advisability of asking the Governor to declare Martial Law and give the National Guard full authority to handle the situation both from the standpoint of evacuation and possible looting. We are to call them back in one hour.

11:15 A.M. - Capt. Cornwall at Jeffersonville at the present time without communication or method of contact with Captain Fleischer. We are now occupying area of about two blocks at north end of Municipal Bridge, all surrounding area under water. Now making patrols by boat thru flooded business district. No looting going on at present. Men have been on duty constantly and are very tired, otherwise they are in good physical condition. River stage 51.6 feet now. Have telephone and boat communication with Jeffersonville Depot. Telephone number is 1936 at Jeffersonville, no trouble getting through to Indianapolis. Someone there all the time.

12:35 P.M. - Wayne Coy reports that evacuation of Jeffersonville Depot is being completed over the B & O R. R., taking 600 to 1000 out of Jeffersonville Depot to Seymour by way of the B&O. Sending 1500 to Charlestown.

Monday, January 25, 1937

4:40 A. M. - Lt. Knaub, Charlestown, Ind. About 750 people there. In 20 minutes will send trucks to edge of water at Jeffersonville to evacuate people there. Sending them north. Have plenty of food. Need field ranges and utensils. Expect number of people to be increased to 1200.

5:28 A. M. - SEYMOUR, Mr. Tilton called reporting: Capable of taking care of 500 people, have rations for 24 hours. Train just left Jeffersonville with 1500 people - will arrive there around 7:00 A.M.

6:15 A. M. - SEYMOUR called General Straub. Train load of refugees enroute from Jeffersonville, 1500 around 7:30 A.M. Don't load them up. Let them take care of just what they can take care of, and send the rest on up to Indianapolis.

6:45 A.M. - CHARLESTOWN, Gen. Cox. Last train out of Depot got into Charlestown at 5:30 A. M. 3 or 4 got off, rest coming toward Indianapolis. Red Cross officers pulling them off. People housed, scattered pretty well. Sending some Field Ranges and Cooking Utensils. Will check G-I cans.

7:50 A. M. - This office called Captain Klepinger at North Vernon who reported they arrived at 2:00 A.M. He requested ointment, ASA compound tablets, laxatives, camphorated oil and cots.

8:45 A.M. - Captain Cornwall at Jeffersonville reported troops located in Administration Building on the Municipal Bridge. Jeffersonville now entirely under water. Transportation by boats only.

Three weeks of high water eroded the ground beneath the Pennsylvania Railroad tracks north of Jeffersonville. Major structural failures destroyed transportation, communication equipment and utility installations. After the '37 Flood, months of work was needed to bring conditions back to operational status.

Postcard Collection – 1990.19.19

11:15 A.M. - The number of homeless people is so enormous that it cannot be estimated. They are evacuating people from their homes. Water is rising at about one inch an hour. The weather is clear but the snow is heavy on the ground. It is beginning to thaw. Going to have to coordinate the boat work. They are going to contact the Coast Guard to see if they will take over that duty and establish a Liaison Officer with them.... Want large size flat boats. Also need boots. The men can not work where they should without the rubber boots.

END OF LOG BOOK

A dentist's office in Jeffersonville shows the devastating effect of weeks of submersion in the cold, muddy flood waters. While many people believed the greatest destruction came from madly rushing currents of water, in truth slow soaking created greater destruction. Building interiors suffered from dissolved plaster, de–composed veneers, soaked wallpaper and warped floorings.

Caufield and Shook Collection – 149412

On January 24, temperatures dipped into the low teens as snow and sleet pelted Louisville. Fourth Street, looking south from York, provides an idea of the frigid conditions faced by rescuers and refugees trying to escape downtown Louisville. Local medical officials predicted 15,000 cases of pneumonia due to the soaking and freezing conditions.

Metropolitan Sewer District Collection — M495

"Black Sunday"

Louisville's "Magic Corner," Fourth Street and Broadway, was flooded on "Black Sunday" when the Brown Hotel saw three and one–half feet of water in its lobby. On this fateful day, power utilities closed and WHAS radio fell silent for 90 minutes. To many Louisvillians, the news of water in the lobby of the Brown Hotel brought home the true threat facing the city.

Caufield and Shook Collection – 149479

January 24, 1937

All of the adverse conditions prevalent in Louisville during the first three weeks of January 1937 were, in many ways, only a prologue to the city's greatest trial – Sunday, January 24 – the day remembered locally as "Black Sunday."

Despite forecasts of clear weather for Sunday, a heavy rain began falling about 2 a.m. The previous night, temperatures had dropped to 18 degrees and the ground froze, which promoted runoff instead of absorption. During that morning, water began covering the corner of Fourth and Broadway, the city's central intersection. Water rose to a depth of three-and-one-half feet in the lobby of the Brown Hotel, and by now, 40 percent of the city was under water. Broadway had become a turbulent stream,

St. Theresa Church, at Schiller and Kentucky, looks like an island as surging waters from Beargrass Creek flooded the streets of the Germantown neighborhood. Over 250 of the city's 300 churches were forced to close, with those on higher grounds becoming important relief and rescue stations. In those Roman Catholic churches that remained above the flood waters, Mass was offered in unheated and darkened sanctuaries.

Goodman-Paxton – Box 6 Item 315

with a forceful current running six miles an hour through the east-west heart of Louisville. Only powerful motor boats with experienced crews were capable of crossing Broadway. The flooding of the central business district symbolized the crisis to native Louisvillians and public morale plummeted when word spread of water in the Brown Hotel.

For the first time during the crisis, drowning deaths and other fatalities were reported. Henry Arnold, 74, died of exposure at the home of his daughter after being rescued in Bullitt County. John Schmidt, 55, of 540 East Walnut was stricken fatally with exposure and exhaustion from relief work. While on a house call one of the city's most eminent physicians, Dr. Morris Flexner, and five patients suffered carbon monoxide poisoning due to a faulty furnace. They all survived.

Churches and synagogues on this Sunday were dark, but not necessarily silent. All pastors of the Louisville

The Basil Doerhoefer Mansion, on West Broadway and Southwestern Parkway, was flooded with only the rooftop of an automobile to indicate the street level. The mansion, originally a private home, was the site of Loretto High School from 1925 until 1974. The grand house, today's Christ Temple Apostolic Church, sits diagonally across Broadway from Shawnee Park.

1937 Ohio River Flood Photograph Collections (Corwin Short Photos) – 2002.010.037

A souvenir post card demonstrates the reason for LG&E's inability to produce enough electricity for tens of thousands of customers. Power supplied by emergency power lines from Central Kentucky's Dix Dam, and generators from local manufacturing plants, allowed hospitals and the telephone company barely enough electricity to maintain the most basic of services.

Postcard Collection – 1990.19.21

Council of Churches were urged to have people available to receive donations of food, clothes and money. The Louisville Conference of Jewish Organizations announced that no worship services would be held. Archbishop John A. Floeresh announced that local Catholic churches would not be heated or lighted for customary Sunday services but, where possible, priests would be in the cold, dark sanctuaries to offer Holy Mass. The archbishop also released Catholics temporarily from the restriction of no meat on Fridays during the crisis. Nearly all denominations provided radio services on Sunday afternoon.

Mayor Neville Miller repeatedly went on the radio to give instructions and, in some cases, to point an accusatory finger. People in the high lying areas were cautioned to stop consuming gasoline by going sight-seeing in their cars, refrain from tying up telephone lines and stop hoarding drinking water. Merchants were sternly warned to avoid profiteering or their stores and inventories would be confiscated. Some stores did not have to worry about these restrictions. The sales of liquors, wines and beer were banned during the crisis.

The Beargrass Creek Gas Plant, north of River Road, was one of the first utility plants to be submerged. Although working with limited capacity, LG&E was able to supply most customers with natural gas throughout the crisis.

Postcard Collection – 1981.43.12

In the West End, marooned families were being rescued at the rate of 100 an hour – 100 families, not individuals. When the flood reached the 52–foot mark, many costly West End homes were invaded by the cold, brown waters. Most of these houses had been built after the 1913 Flood and had never before experienced high water.

Captain Walter Farrell, Coast Guard commander of Life Saving Station Number 10, identified Jeffersonville as the most dangerous location, and to cross the river meant braving a seven–mile–per–hour current. The Coast Guard had four power boats borrowed from local residents. Skilled rivermen, whose trade was still being practiced at the Falls, were at a premium, but other areas of expertise were also needed. The Department of Welfare issued a call for a dozen experienced business executives to help coordinate volunteer work.

Throughout this terrible Sunday, the city's power plants were dropping off the power grid as generators became submerged. Despite frantic and heroic efforts to keep the great boilers free of water, the record–breaking flooding was shutting down power sources. The LG&E Western Substation went down first, ending all electrical service to the West End. Next, the Canal Station, and then the Riverside Substation, were blacked out, shutting off all street lights in the city. Only a high tension line from central Kentucky's Dix Dam furnished limited wattage to hospitals and the telephone company. Louisville sat in darkness as rain continued to fall.

Streets in the downtown area were deserted. The area around the Louisville Free Public Library was closed, and the famous statue of Abraham Lincoln on the Library grounds saw water rise to Honest Abe's knees. A reporter commented that downtown Louisville had the aspect of a ghost town.

"All lights were out; vehicular traffic was at a minimum; pedestrians crunched along on the sleet–covered sidewalks, silent, wondering. Gone was the usual jam of motors, street cars, taxicabs."

"Black Sunday" was Louisville's day of despair. Local officials and services had reached the point of exhaustion. Desperate rescue efforts were continuing to get people out of low–lying levels in the West End and to safety in the Highlands or out of town. The Red Cross was scrambling to give typhoid injections – sometimes on roof tops or even in the rescue boats. The rain did not stop.

On this Sunday, the temper and courage of Louisville were most strongly tried. People were wet, cold, tired and hungry: tens of thousands had been displaced from their homes and many families were separated, with no knowledge of the fate of missing members; the people who were generously housing refugees were crowded and inconvenienced; the closing of factories and workplaces had stopped most people's pay checks; refugees were suffering from influenza, pneumonia and adverse reactions to the painful typhoid injections; children were gripped by a combination of insecurity, fear and boredom. At this critical time, Louisville believed it had reached the bottom of its suffering – but an additional burden was still to be added.

The emotional nadir of the Great Flood came at 11:35 p.m., when WHAS Radio fell silent due to a loss of electrical power. Now, in addition to all the other trials, contact with the outside world was eliminated. It was the time of gloom and a growing fear of isolation and abandonment.

1937 Ohio River Flood Photograph Collections – 1990.29.38

1937 Ohio River Flood Photograph Collections (Corwin Short Photos) – 2002.010.085

Photos of people, standing in front of their West End shotgun houses, reveal white and African–American families waiting to evacuate their homes. The rapidly–rising water caught many people unprepared to move, and they were forced to escape with little more than the clothes they were wearing.

"Lincoln Standing on Water," one of the most famous images associated with the 1937 Flood, is a bit of an illusion. The photo was taken several days after the flood's crest, when the water had lowered to the feet of the statue. Located at Fourth and York streets, oil streaks on the walls of the Louisville Free Public Library indicate the high water mark actually reached to Lincoln's knees.

Caufield and Shook Collection – 195425

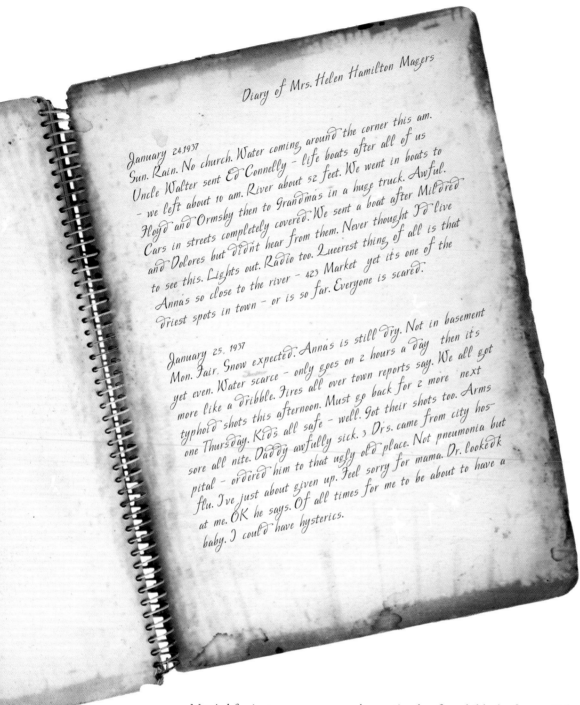

Diary of Mrs. Helen Hamilton Magers

January 24, 1937
Sun. Rain. No church. Water coming around the corner this am.
Uncle Walter sent Ed Connelly - life boats after all of us
- we left about 10 am. River about 52 feet. We went in boats to
Floyd and Ormsby then to Grandma's in a huge truck. Awful.
Cars in streets completely covered. We sent a boat after Mildred
and Dolores but didn't hear from them. Never thought I'd live
to see this. Lights out. Radio too. Queerest thing of all is that
Anna's so close to the river - 423 Market yet it's one of the
driest spots in town - or is so far. Everyone is scared.

January 25, 1937
Mon. Fair. Snow expected. Anna's is still dry. Not in basement
yet even. Water scarce - only goes on 2 hours a day then it's
more like a dribble. Fires all over town reports say. We all got
typhoid shots this afternoon. Must go back for 2 more next
one Thursday. Kids all safe - well. Got their shots too. Arms
sore all nite. Daddy awfully sick. 3 Dr's. came from city hospital - ordered him to that ugly old place. Not pneumonia but
flu. I've just about given up. Feel sorry for mama. Dr. looked
at me. OK he says. Of all times for me to be about to have a
baby. I could have hysterics.

Married for just over one year and expecting her first child, the former Helen Hamilton and her husband H.G. "Duke" (Vonderheide) Magers were residents of the Shelby Park neighborhood. They were evacuated by boat and truck to the home of her grandmother, Brigid Haney Farrell, who lived in the Guthrie-Coke Apartments – a then dry area of downtown – on Chestnut between Third and Fourth streets.

Helen's uncle was Walter Farrell, commander of the U.S. Coast Guard Station in Louisville, and a second generation riverman. His father, Edmund J. "Ed" Farrell, served as an original crew member of U.S. Life Saving Station #10 when the station was first established to guard the Falls of the Ohio in 1881. The former Coast Guard station, commissioned in 1929 and the third to serve that purpose, is now known as the Mayor *Andrew Broaddus* and houses the administrative offices for the *Belle of Louisville*.

Like many Louisvillians following the 1937 Flood who would seek higher ground in the eastern sections of the city, the Magers family permanently relocated to St. Matthews.

Within 90 minutes of going silent, the familiar voice of WHAS returned to the airways with emergency power being supplied by Kentucky Utilities. Also, the messages from the WHAS staff were being telephoned to other radio stations for re–broadcast to Louisville. The Fall Cities forever owe a debt of gratitude to the generous service of stations in Nashville, Indianapolis, Covington and Lexington. These re–broadcasts helped buoy spirits and lift morale. Louisvillians discovered they were not alone.

President Franklin Roosevelt addressed the nation and asked for support for the Red Cross. Almost immediately over $2,000,000 was given in response. To solicit local donations, Mayor Miller established a volunteer committee consisting of important community leaders, including: J. McFerran Barr, chairman; William C. Dabney, John G. Heyburn, Preston P. Joyes, David Maloney, Rabbi Joseph Rauch, Mrs. Louis Seelbach and Prentiss M. Terry. Within 90 minutes, the committee had collected nearly $7,000.

Even as "Black Sunday" faded into history, the trial of the Great Flood had not ended, for the water continued to rise.

"A story of magnificent struggle against overwhelming odds."

The first Flood Edition of the *Courier–Journal* and *Times*, published on Monday, January 25, related a story of epic struggle to maintain electrical service at the Waterside Plant. Although tinged by racial attitudes of the era, the vivid depiction of LG&E employees is a testament to bravery and responsibility. Selected highlights of the lead article "Louisville In Dark As Walls Crumble At Riverside Plant" tell a story of courage and sacrifice.

Ends Magnificent Struggle

The failure of the waterside plant wrote a disheartening but inevitable finale to a story of magnificent struggle against overwhelming odds.

More than 200 men, all extra help, have worked night and day barricading doors and windows, caulking wall breaks and splits in the floor, all at extreme danger to their lives.

Singing spirituals, giant Negroes labored with the sweat running down their backs and chins. As the cracks opened in the walls, they set braces unshrinkingly and piled sandbags in place.

They sang and joked together, almost contemptuous of the threatening vast bulk of water looming high above their heads.

A dynamo pit was 300 feet below the river level, and workmen manned it too. Water from above trickled down upon them, but they stuck to their jobs.

January 25–27, 1937

Monday morning, January 25, began clear and sunny – the first of three days of no rain. By this time the city had reached the end of its resources and local services were exhausted. Mayor Neville Miller asked that martial law be declared. Miller called Kentucky Governor A.B. Chandler, who contacted President Roosevelt. Martial law was declared immediately and the nation responded to Louisville's call for help.

EXECUTIVE ORDER AND PROCLAMATION.

WHEREAS, the Honorable Neville Miller is the duly elected, qualified and acting Mayor of the City of Louisville, Jefferson County, Kentucky, and the chief executive of said city; and,

WHEREAS, approximately two-thirds of the area of said city is now submerged in the greatest flood in the history of said city and approximately two hundred thousand residents of said city reside in the flooded area; and,

WHEREAS, the said Neville Miller, Mayor of the City of Louisville, had advised the Governor of the Commonwealth of Kentucky that the civil officers and agencies of the city of Louisville are unable to protect the health, lives, and property of the inhabitants and residents of said city during this emergency and that the aid of the military forces is necessary and imperative, and has requested the Governor of the Commonwealth of Kentucky to declare martial law and request that Federal troops be sent to the City of Louisville to aid and assist in protecting the health, lives and property of the residents and citizens of said city; and,

WHEREAS, the Governor of the Commonwealth of Kentucky is fully informed and knows of the imperative need of centralized direction of all forces, civil and military, to aid in rescuing the citizens and residents of the City of Louisville in the flooded area and in protecting the health, lives, and property of said citizens and residents:

NOW, THEREFORE, The Premises of all Considered, It is Ordered and Directed by the Governor of the Commonwealth of Kentucky that martial law be and the same hereby is proclaimed for the entire city of Louisville, and the Honorable Neville Miller, Mayor of the City of Louisville, hereby is designated as Provost Marshal to be in Supreme charge and direction of all civil and military authorities and agencies in the city of Louisville, and he is hereby vested with full power to command and direct said forces and all of them in rescuing people from the flooded area and moving them to places of safety, in preserving peace, and in protecting the health, lives and property of the citizens and residents of the City of Louisville, and to issue and enforce such orders, commands, rules and regulations as may be proper, expedient and necessary to accomplish the ends aforesaid.

It is further ordered and directed by the Governor of the Commonwealth of Kentucky that Colonel Sidney R. Smith, Commanding Officer of all companies and divisions of the National Guard and the military forces which are or may be assigned to duty in the City of Louisville, and said Colonel Sidney R. Smith will work in coordination with and under the orders and directions of the said Neville Miller as Provost Marshal in directing all of said military forces.

This order and proclamation shall be and remain in full force and effect until modified or terminated by further executive order and proclamation of the Governor of the Commonwealth of Kentucky.

Given under my hand as Governor of the Commonwealth of Kentucky at Frankfort, Kentucky, this January 25, 1937.

Governor of the Commonwealth of Kentucky
Albert Benjamin Chandler

President Roosevelt responded immediately and announced that the White House would operate on a 24–hour war–time basis, with the president receiving continual updates on the crisis. On that Monday, 500 soldiers from Ft. Knox were rushed to Louisville to aid flood victims and keep order. Bowman Field, its runways now beginning to dry since the rain had halted, was used as their headquarters and an estimated 200,000 pounds of supplies were flown in to this site. During the Great Flood, over 3,000 refugees were flown out of Bowman Field. Over 20 percent of the U.S. Coast Guard's personnel were rushed to Louisville to conduct lifesaving missions. U.S. Navy personnel from the Great Lakes and North Carolina were brought in to help evacuate water–bound citizens.

Downtown Louisville had become practically an island, bounded by Main on the north, Broadway on the south, Shelby on the east and 18th Street on the west. City Hall was protected from the continually rising waters by sandbags and pumps. The Jefferson County Court House (now Louisville Metro Hall) and Armory (now Louisville Gardens) provided thousands of refugees with their first touch of warmth, comfort and safety. Over 75,000 refugees would be processed in the halls of the old Armory.

The declaration of Martial Law allowed federal help to pour into Louisville. Soldiers from Fort Knox, members of the Kentucky National Guard and one–fifth of the U.S. Coast Guard were rapidly deployed to provide security, rescue crews and traffic control.

1937 Ohio River Flood Photograph Collections (Corwin Short Photos) – 2002.010.014

Downtown Louisville became an island, with only a few streets in the central business district elevated enough to remain relatively dry. Basements were drowned, and only continual pumping allowed boilers and heating systems to remain functional. Citizens Union National Bank (now Kentucky Home Life Building), located on the northeast corner of Jefferson and Fifth streets, used a row of gasoline–powered pumps to remain operable.

R.G. Potter Collection – 3470

Louisville's grand City Hall (on Sixth Street, looking north), built in the early 1870s, was the center for coordination of all relief, rescue and rehabilitation efforts. Mayor Miller put the building, and the entire apparatus of local government, on a twenty–four hour operating schedule. The building originally housed the offices of the Mayor and the Board of Aldermen. With the creation of the merged Louisville–Jefferson County government, the Italianate–Second Empire structure now provides offices for the Louisville Metro Council.

City Hall. R.G. Potter Collection – 538.1

The basement of City Hall was sandbagged to repel the encroaching waters that stopped just short of the building. The basement was pumped for 260 consecutive hours to allow the heating plant to operate.

Caufield and Shook Collection – 149475

Pepper Island

Shortly after the '37 Flood, a perceptive teacher at Shawnee (Girls) High School assigned her students the duty of writing essays based on their personal flood experiences. She collected them in a small book called "Flood Stories." Excerpts from the essay written by Virginia Austin, of 403 North 34th Street, recall her own island in the Portland neighborhood:

...we were told not to be alarmed because we were high and dry. I went to bed thinking that the water would never get us, but I was surprised the next morning because the water was beginning to cover our street.

All of us helped to carry upstairs a ton and half of coal which was put in our used–to–be– kitchen....We put the washer in the bathroom and filled it with water from the faucets – with clear water which was becoming scarce.

After we had put everything in order upstairs, we began living a life that we had never lived before. We were on an island which covered the whole square from Alford to Jewell Avenue. There were ten houses on one side of the island and a commons on the other side.

In order to save coal oil, we would retire early. This coal oil was given to us by the Kentucky Consumers Oil Company at 37th and Parker Avenue. They were afraid to leave the coal oil and gasoline around the plant because it endangered their lives and the lives of the people on the two islands.

After the water had risen sufficiently, various things began to float down the street. The first thing we fished out of the water was a barrel of Red Pickled Peppers. Apparently, these peppers came from Von Allman Preserving Company at 33rd and Bank Streets, which lost a great deal of their merchandise.

The next day we fished out several more barrels of peppers, so we named our island Pepper Island.

The Federal Works Progress Administration (WPA) provided remarkable public services during the Flood crisis. The WPA hired 6,650 local workers to assist in rescues, food preparation, deliveries and hundreds of other duties. The workers were paid $30 a month, a salary that relieved the crushing economic plight caused by the Great Depression, and allowed a decent living wage for participants in the program.

1937 Ohio River Flood Photograph Collections – 2001.041.31

The Brinly–Hardy Company has produced quality plows and farm equipment for five generations in Louisville. Located at the corner of Main and Preston streets, the company's shipping warehouse was converted into Louisville Slugger Field in 1998. The entire playing field of today's stadium was underwater during the '37 Flood.

Preston and Main. Postcard Collection – 1999.63.19

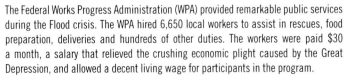

Two tent cities were constructed almost overnight by the WPA. Due to policies of legal segregation, two separate tent communities were created. A tent city on Algonquin Parkway was the home of 850 white refugees, and 1,200 African–Americans were housed at George Rogers Clark Park on Poplar Level Road. The American Red Cross supplied the tent cities with food, medical services, clothing and supplies.

R.G. Potter Collection – 572

The WPA operated a health clinic in the Snead Building to dispense medicines and provide primary treatment options. An aggressive local public health program, stressing inoculations and other preventive measures, hindered the outbreak of any serious infectious diseases.

1937 Ohio River Flood Photograph Collections – 2001.041.86

The Federal Works Progress Administration (WPA) hired 6,650 local workers to aid in flood relief. Two tent cities were built by the WPA for refugees. The facilities were segregated, with 800 white citizens housed in the tent city on Algonquin Parkway, and 1,200 African–Americans put up in the tent city at George Rogers Clark Park on Poplar Level Road. The operation and maintenance of the tent cities were the responsibility of the American Red Cross. Eventually, the WPA supplied 15,000 workers to Kentucky and provided over 1.5 million dollars in supplies.

The WPA also took over the Fire Department's responsibility of pumping out basements. The workers maintained pumps in the Brown Hotel for 563 hours and at City Hall for 260 hours. WPA workers also removed and buried dead livestock and animals in the city and county in six–foot–deep trenches. The WPA buried over 3,000 horses, mules and cows, 4,000 sheep and hogs, and 7,500 small animals – chickens, dogs and cats.

The American Red Cross performed heroic service all through the flooded Ohio and Mississippi river valleys and was especially active in Louisville. At the beginning of the Great Flood, the Red Cross had a local staff of 30 people, but before the disaster had passed, over 1,600 Red Cross workers were present. During the crisis the Red Cross inoculated

The American Red Cross, working with Louisville Board of Health personnel, administered an estimated 220,000 inoculations of typhoid serum. The largest peacetime public health effort ever mounted until that time, local Red Cross personnel rose from 30 before the Flood, to 1,600 during the crisis.

1937 Ohio River Flood Photograph Collections – 1990.29.41

220,000 people for typhoid. They were providing hot meals and relief for 230,000 a day. The citizens of the United States donated over 25 million dollars in flood relief for the Ohio Valley.

Each Red Cross staff member served an average caseload of 177 people. In the course of the Ohio–Mississippi Rivers Flood of 1937, six American Red Cross workers lost their lives.

In addition to assistance from the federal government, dozens of American cities and towns rallied to Louisville's aid. Police and firemen from around the nation were sent to help. Boston, Philadelphia, Trenton and Chicago supplied hundreds of policemen to maintain order. More than 70 communities sent at least one policeman, and the Pendennis Club was commandeered to house many of the visiting officers.

Troops from the National Guard patrolled the East End in armored cars. Two hundred and seventy–three policemen had already arrived and were detailed to provide security in the East End, by now the only densely–populated part of the city. A plane load of officers landed from Philadelphia announcing that an additional 125 were on their way. A policeman's inn was established in the I.M. Bloom School on Lucia Avenue near Bardstown Road, and to that location reported an unusual national blend of law enforcement officers. Pittsburgh supplied 21 men and a physician, while the Pennsylvania State

WPA workers performed one of the grim tasks during, and after, the flood crisis. Over 3,000 large farm animals were buried in mass graves, while thousands of smaller animals and pets were also interred. A mule was discovered suspended in a tree 42 feet above the ground on the farm of W. B. Terry on Lower River Road.

Caufield and Shook Collection – 150554

Mayor Neville Miller inspects the long blue line of Pennsylvania State Police in the Highlands. Many visiting policemen from other cities were housed in the I.N. Bloom School on Lucia Avenue. Pennsylvania sent over 100 officers to help provide security in the Highlands and Crescent Hill, the most densely–populated areas of Louisville during relief activities.

Courier-Journal and Louisville Times

Police sent 30 men initially, and followed up with 70 more. They provided security at St. James Church, located at the corner of Bardstown Road and Edenside Avenue.

The Maryland State Police sent three men; Syracuse, N.Y., five men; Bristol, Virginia–Tennessee, five men; Atlanta, three policemen; Boston, 21 men; and Champaign, Illinois, Cold Water, Michigan, South Haven, Michigan and Johnson City, Tennessee, two men each. Two more were on their way from Duluth, Minnesota. Chicago detailed 43, while far–off Phoenix assigned two men.

Henry Ford announced he was shipping two train loads of relief supplies to the city. Lighting equipment was enroute from Detroit, courtesy of the Dodge Motors plant. Mayor LaGuardia of New York City detailed a crew of sanitation engineers to share their expertise and advice on cleaning the streets. Former Louisvillian and pioneering film director D. W. Griffith sent a check for $100 and apologized that his reduced state of wealth would not allow more.

Help began arriving, but Louisvillians still conducted the bulk of emergency services. Even after martial law was declared, all administrative decisions were under the control of Mayor and now Provost Marshal Neville Miller, and Louisville's civilian volunteers and government.

The Kentucky State Board of Health rented rooms in the Louisville Hotel to serve as their temporary headquarters. A loaf of Louisville's Honey Krust Bread shares office space in their impromptu kitchen and administrative center.

Caufield and Shook Collection – 149598

Mayor Names Citizen Bodies To Direct Help
Committees Given Authority to Handle Problem of Flood.

Courier–Journal and *Times*
January 26, 1937

Mayor Neville Miller Monday night announced the outline of his relief organization. It follows:
1 – Co–ordinating committee, City attorney's office, City Hall, telephone JA 1920 or WA 2251, extension 228.
Chairman: M. W. Lewis; O.C. Dewey, G. R. Churchill and R. G. Gordon.

Has Full Authority

Subject to approval of the Mayor or his representative, this committee has supervision of work of all other committees, and may take such action as may be necessary to make their work effective.
2 – Outside supply committee, Room 311 City Hall, Wabash 2251. William B. Harrison, chairman, with the remainder of committee to be appointed.
This committee was organized to handle:
(A) – Proffers of supplies; personnel and other contacts from outside committee and individuals; and
(B) – To ascertain from various departments of the organization their requirements for the items listed in (A).

Has Full List

This committee has a full list of proffers as made and has addressed in memorandums to other committees as to their specific requirements.
This committee will co–operate with the transportation committee in moving such supplies.

Food and Health

Housing, Food and Health Committee – Law Department, 1st Floor. Telephone WA 2251–Extension 245.

Chairman: Saunders Jones, Dr. Hugh R. Leavell, John Richardson, McFerran Barr.

Sub–committees:

A – Housing, Highlands. Hartford Smith, Chairman, HI 1579; Frank D. Rash, Prentice M. Terry, L. D. Green, Wallace Davis.

In charge of welfare: Wallace Davis

In charge of health: Dr. Ed Humphrey, T. P. Taylor, Jr.; Harold Miller.

Crescent Hill: John Miller, Vertner D. Smith

South Louisville: Alex Booth, W. I. Wymond.

Downtown: McFarran Barr, J. W. Brown.

Food: R. W. Englehard, Yancey Altsheler.

Red Cross: Charles G. Middleton, Captain Shea

Health: Dr. Hugh Leavell, Dr. Olson.

Transportation Group.

Transportation Location 2d floor, City Hall Annex Telephone JA 5401. Chairman, William C. Dabney. This committee is in charge of all transportation including (A) Trucks Sub–committees Lew Ulrich, Al Rosenberg.

This transportation committee has charge of rationing of gasoline. (B) Boats Subcommittee, James Courtney, James Dorman.

(C) Bridges Sub–committee, William Hoge.

(D) Labor, Sub–committee, Gene Sturges.

(E) Railroads, Sub–committee: A. J. Knessey.

Evacuation Body

The foregoing transportation committee will have charge of acceptances of offers of transportation facilities and of dispatching and control of those facilities.

Evacuation Committee – Location. Aldermen's chamber, Telephone JA 7733.

Chairman, Col. George Cheschire, Assistants Major Watson, Captain Raymond.

(A) Water Rescue – Maj. Earl Major.

(B) Transportation – Owen Voight, (1) truck (2) boat, (3) rail; (C) medical, Ray Kirchdorfer

(D) Housing – John Dodd.

The duties of this committee are to arrange to pick up and rescue persons in West End where there are more than fifty in one concentrated area. This organization works in connection with transportation, medical and housing and has representative from these committees available at his desk.

All previous instructions from the Mayor's office as to organization are now to be disregarded.

This organization is now in full effect.

The Pontoon Bridge transported refugees from downtown Louisville to the edge of the turbulent stream that was Beargrass Creek. The western entrance to the bridge started at 915 East Jefferson Street. The one-way bridge moved living, and dead, citizens toward temporary quarters on Bardstown Road.

1937 Ohio River Flood Photograph Collections - 1986.56.8

The safety of the Highlands lay at the eastern end of the Pontoon Bridge. The bridge, which stretched from 915 East Jefferson to Baxter And Barret, was the creation of ingenious local engineers and carpenters, and remains one of Louisville's most enduring flood traditions. During its four days of operation, an estimated 75,000 persons crossed the six–block–long buoyant bridge.

Caulfield and Shook Collection – 149543 1/2

The Buoyant Bridge to Safety

One of the brightest spots of Louisville's Great Flood experience was the imagination and ingenuity displayed by people involved in the local relief effort. It was a time when local problems were solved by local solutions – some solutions that would only be possible in Louisville, Kentucky.

One of the enduring images of the '37 Flood was the construction of the famous pontoon bridge made of empty whiskey barrels. Its purpose was to assist the removal of downtown refugees and transport them to safety in the relief stations of the Highlands and Crescent Hill. To span the turbulent current of Beargrass Creek, local engineers and architects constructed an 1,800–foot floating bridge from 919 East Jefferson Street to Baxter Avenue and Lexington Road. An East End distillery provided 1,400 unused barrels to provide ballast to the pontoon bridge. Construction of the bridge began at 9 a.m. on January 26 and was completed before the end of the day.

Local architect and reserve officer, Captain W. S. Arrasmith, designed the bridge and recruited 300 workers. Skilled carpenters and problem–solvers, the crew labored all night – often immersed in cold flood waters up to their waists.

The Pontoon Bridge received its buoyancy from 1,400 new oaken bourbon barrels donated by an unknown East End distillery. Each refugee was instructed to leave ten feet of space between themselves, and walk in the center of the bridge. The three-foot-wide Pontoon Bridge was secured to telephone poles for stability. The terminus was on Baxter Avenue, between Lexington Road and Barret, just west of the Town Talk Caps Company. Almost all of the buildings shown are still present 70 years later.

Royal Photo Studio Collection - 50312.00

Return over pontoon bridge thrown together, I hear, in 23 hours by capable W. S. Arrasmith at one end and Danish Wiesa at other. Volunteers, lawyers, and such–like, do carpentering. Fine job.

Lessons of interdependence. Not of rugged individualism. Were they aiding kin, friends? Not at all. They aided, rescued, protected strangers. It made no sort of difference. Those who stood in icy waters, arm–pit deep, to build a bridge they weren't going to travel over it. An outpouring of man to man. Sacrifice, service, for others.

Leaves from a Diary by E. A. Jonas

The workers built wooden cages containing three empty wooden whiskey barrels. These cages were joined together and secured to telephone poles. A narrow wooden walkway with handrails was constructed on top of the floating cages. Lighting was provided and evacuees were cautioned to allow 10 feet of space between themselves, and to walk in the very center of the bridge that led in only one direction – one–way east.

On its first day of service 35,000 refugees, the population of a small city, crossed the bridge to the Highlands. It is estimated that during its four days of existence, over 75,000 made their way carefully over the lurching, rolling pontoon bridge. At times the process of evacuating the living gave way to moving the dead. A fleet of ambulances and hearses waited at the Baxter Avenue end of the bridge as 11 dead, two of them babies, were transported from the City Hospital to Cave Hill Cemetery for burial or to the temporary morgue at the Highland Chevrolet Garage (northeast corner of Bardstown Road and Grinstead Drive).

April 8, 1937

Miss Helen Randolph,
Apt. #3, 239 E. Gray St.
Louisville, KY.

My dear Miss Randolph:

Complying with your telephone request, I am furnishing you herewith such information as I possess on the improvised floating footbridge which was constructed in Louisville for evacuation purposes during the recent flood.

During the morning of January 25th, Captain W.S. Arrasmith, 380th Engineers, of this city and another engineer from the City Hall whose name I don't recall, met me in my office and we discussed the practicability of constructing such a bridge. As there was no shortage of the essential materials and labor the project was clearly feasible and these two gentlemen undertook the design and preparation of such detailed plans as were essential…

As to the actual design, the buoyant force was furnished by whiskey kegs (50 gal. capacity, as I recall). The supports for the bridge were made by enclosing 3 of these kegs in a crate. I believe these supports were placed about 10 feet apart. Upon the crates were placed sections of duck board to provide the walkway and a handrail. The walkway was designed to be 3 feet wide in order that the superimposed load might be concentrated near the center of the floats. Later on this width was increased to about 5 feet by carpenters from the Tennessee Valley Authority. This destroyed to a considerable extent its original lateral stability and the resulting oscillation caused by the motion of people on the bridge would probably have caused a rapid disintegration. Fortunately, by this time the need for the bridge was nearly over.

I have no knowledge of the actual construction but understand that the labor used was picked up locally from carpenters out of work because of the flood. If additional information is desired and you are unable to contact Captain Arrasmith, I suggest that you communicate with Captain Homer Puckett, 380th Engineers, who, I am informed, also assisted in supervising the construction.

Very truly yours,

S. J. Horn,
Captain, Corps of Engineers,
Military Assistant

On February 9, after the Flood had receded, this photo provides a detailed look at the Pontoon Bridge's construction. Three 50–gallon whiskey barrels were boxed in simple wooden frames and a walkway and hand–rails were added. The sections were joined together by men working in the frigid water up to the shoulders, "to build a bridge they were never going to travel over."

1937 Ohio River Flood Photograph Collections – 1986.56.7

St. Aloysius, on Payne Street near Baxter, was one of the smallest parishes in the city. Ironically, upon it fell one of the heaviest burdens. St. Aloysius was the first stop for thousands of refugees crossing the pontoon bridge. Early Sunday, January 24, the church gave shelter to 30 refugee families of their own parish. Hundreds of the workers who put up the pontoon bridge and 30 members of the Glasgow, Kentucky National Guard found food and shelter at St. Aloysius. The men of the parish looked after the supplies and the refugees while the women of the church organized themselves into three shifts. They cooked and served hot meals continuously day and night for approximately 20,000 persons.

The C. C. Mengel Company, makers of fine furniture and pianos, offered to build emergency rescue boats for the flood effort. Col. Charles C. Mengel III, the company president, told his workers to make the boats out of the best materials available. The Mengel craftsmen, working all night, produced 100 john–boats. The boats, four feet wide and 20 feet long, were constructed of the finest solid mahogany. Mahogany was used because of its fine grain and lack of knot holes.

When completed, the boats' seaworthiness was tested in the flood waters surrounding the plant. If the boat did not leak it was released for rescue duty. The Mengel john–boats had room for 12 persons or could carry two tons of food. Each boat

Col. Charles C. Mengel III, president of the Mengel Company, ordered his skilled craftsmen to build 100 large john–boats to aid in the rescue efforts. He selected mahogany as the best possible building material for the boats. A rare and expensive wood, mahogany was usually reserved for pianos and fine furniture, but Col. Mengel believed that nothing but the best would do for rescue work.

Herald-Post – 2713

cost approximately $30 to construct, a figure about four times greater than boats made of more common material. These were surely the most elegant john–boats ever constructed and only 20 were returned after the Great Flood. The beautiful mahogany was not salvageable.

The Henry Vogt Machine Company volunteered their facility to the flood effort and their power plant to provide emergency service to hospitals and local bakeries. Their contribution, while limited by the size of their plant, proved to be critical to maintaining basic human services.

The grand Seelbach Hotel offered amenities that were unavailable from any other downtown host. Electrical service was out at every other hotel and guests were forced to climb dozens of floors to reach their unheated rooms. The Seelbach had always maintained a private large–scale generator and boasted its own artesian water well in the basement. The rooms were unlit and unheated, but they did deliver a degree of comfort to their guests.

A local social service agency, Neighborhood House, located at 428 South First Street, was normally a site of community help, educational and recreational programs. During the flood crisis, Neighborhood House was asked to provide hot meals to City Hall and other relief stations downtown. They would eventually serve over 45,000 hot meals and spread their operation into the neighboring Miller's Cafeteria and the kitchen at Christ Church Cathedral. After refrigerators and freezers lost their electricity, the Pendennis Club donated hoards of delicacies, including lobsters, steaks, caviar and crab. At times, relief meals from Neighborhood House resembled fine dining in the Oak Room of the Seelbach Hotel.

Not everyone in town was eating lobster and caviar. Racial segregation was both a custom, and the law, of the land. While many examples of generosity and cooperation between blacks and whites were manifested throughout the '37 Flood, the institutional separation of the races caused constant concern for officials during the crisis. This separation was especially pronounced in the careful establishment of racially–divided relief centers and residences. A January 28 story in the *Courier*, "Negroes Get Attention in Lexington" illustrates the extra lengths government and public service agencies went to insure the social norm would not be disturbed.

Some fortunate African–American refugees were housed in relative comfort in the Presbyterian Colored Mission at Hancock and Jefferson streets. Segregation laws of the times separated the races into designated relief areas. Many officials and agencies objected to the arbitrary segregation policies and thought that they needlessly interfered with the effort to save lives.

Caufield and Shook Collection – 149346

Approximately 200 Negro refugees from Louisville arrived in Lexington Tuesday night, and Wednesday approximately seventy–five white refugees had been placed in private homes in Lexington. Negro refugees were cleared through the Colored Community Center, inoculated for typhoid fever and placed in Negro churches, the First Baptist Church, the Main Street Baptist Church and St. Andrew's Hall, Fourth and Upper.

Mayor Neville Miller of Louisville asked Mayor E. Reed Wilson how many Negro refugees the city could handle. This immediately led to the consolidation of the many Negro committees that have already been working in flood relief, and R. H. Hogan, Judson King and Ages Brant were selected to head the consolidated committee.

Mayor Wilson was notified by telephone that as soon as a train carrying 1,000 refugees to Shelbyville returned to Louisville, it would be loaded with Negro refugees and sent here.

WORLD'S HIGHEST STAN

There's no wa like the American W

Refugees were cared for in primitive conditions at the Progress School in Lyndon. The WPA maintained this center, and other relief sites, providing rudimentary shelter, food and medicine to growing numbers of evacuated citizens. During the crisis, large numbers of Louisvillians were sent by train to African–American churches in Lexington.

1937 Ohio River Flood Photograph Collections – 2001.041.09

People were cared for, no matter their race or creed. On many occasions, people of both races were brought together by circumstances and inter–racial friendships began. For a period of time, the Great Flood served as a great social leveler as everyone was the same color – muddy; everyone felt the same emotion – fear; and everyone shared the same dream – a return to normalcy.

Louisville's East End was especially welcoming to people in need. One private home in Crescent Hill extended its hospitality to 22 refugees. St. Francis of Assisi School on Bardstown Road, a clearing house for refugees, housed as many as 325 at one time. They provided hot food and clothing to approximately 2,500. A doctor and nurses were in attendance at all times, and the vaccination clinic gave some 10,000 typhoid shots.

More than 3,000 African–Americans and 1,500 white persons were housed in private homes in the Highlands. From Crescent Hill, 600 African–Americans were moved to the Lincoln Institute near Shelbyville, while several hundred more were housed at the Emmet Field School. Every day they stayed at the school, the refugees held daily church services. On one occasion the preacher chose as his subject, "Noah's Ark."

The *LIFE* magazine edition of February 1, 1937 carried a photo that is a classic iconic image of the Great Depression, an indelible statement of irony and racial division. A queue of weary African–Americans are shown waiting in a food line on the sidewalk next to Broadway Liquors at 13th and Broadway. Plastered on the wall behind them is a billboard depicting a happy middle–class white family – Dad, Mom, Junior, Sis and their shaggy dog – enjoying a drive. The message of the billboard proclaims *"There's no way like the American Way* – WORLD'S HIGHEST STANDARD OF LIVING." This powerful photograph was taken by Margaret Bourke–White.

The First Lady of News Photography

Margaret Bourke–White was an American original. One of the best early photojournalists, "Peg" Bourke–White became one of the first media superstars. Publisher Henry R. Luce admired her industrial photography and hired her for his new publication, *Fortune* magazine. When Luce created *LIFE* magazine in 1936, Bourke–White was one of the original four staff photographers and took the first photo to ever grace the cover of the magazine.

A keen observer, Bourke–White traveled to Russia to document the growth of the Soviet system, created lasting images of Mahatma Gandhi and photographed diamond miners in South Africa. In January 1937, she was assigned coverage of Louisville's flood crisis for *LIFE*. Her indelible image of weary African–Americans standing in a bread line was instantly recognized as a classic news photo.

LIFE magazine photographer Margaret Bourke–White recruited local photographer Corwin Short to be her guide during her assignment at the Louisville flood. "Peg" Bourke–White is shown doing her job, going to extreme measures to provide classic images of American photojournalism. She is shown climbing out of a second–story window at 33rd and Rudd Avenue in Portland.

Mayor's Scrapbook – Page 16

Bourke–White enlisted local photographer Corwin Short to accompany her during the Louisville assignment. Short's own collection of photographs of their work together during the '37 Flood, donated to the University of Louisville Photographic Archives in 2002, demonstrate Bourke–White's daring, energy and dedication to capturing her subject no matter what conditions she faced. The hand–written captions on the photos, often light–hearted and humorous, show the resilience of the human spirit in the face of disaster. Most of these images have never before been published, and provide a rare portfolio of American news photography and intimate portraits of Louisville during the Great Flood.

On January 26, the city faced another brush with disaster. A serious fire broke out at the factory of the Louisville Varnish Company at 14th and Maple Streets belonging to industrialist Col. P. H. Callahan. It was feared that burning varnish would spread over the flood waters and burn down Louisville, but firemen, working in water six feet deep, were able to dynamite the buildings and prevent its spread. The fire did more than $500,000 in damage and resulted in three deaths, but it could have been much worse. The fire was visible all over Louisville and many reported thinking it was the end of the world.

Despite the great danger of fire caused by spreading oil and gasoline, Louisville experienced only 185 fires during the '37 Flood, only about one–half the usual total for the same time period. Cincinnati suffered a much greater fire during its 1937 flood, a 10–alarm fire which caused over $3 million dollars in damages.

Several other fires occurred during the flood, including a blast and fire which did over $50,000 damage to the Bollinger–Hancock Coffee Company at 115 North Fifth Street. When the platform of the Illinois Central became engulfed in flames, Louisville firemen were forced to simply watch because they could not get near enough to fight the fire. Captain S. G. Render, assistant chief of the fire division, collapsed from exhaustion, but returned to duty the next day.

Following weeks of rain and rising waters, the Great Flood finally crested at 2:00 a.m. on January 27. By 3:00 a.m., the water began to recede. The crest was 57.15 feet, more than 29 feet over flood stage and ten feet higher than the previous record.

The crest of the flood, and the sure knowledge it was beginning to recede, provided a much–needed boost to the exhausted population.

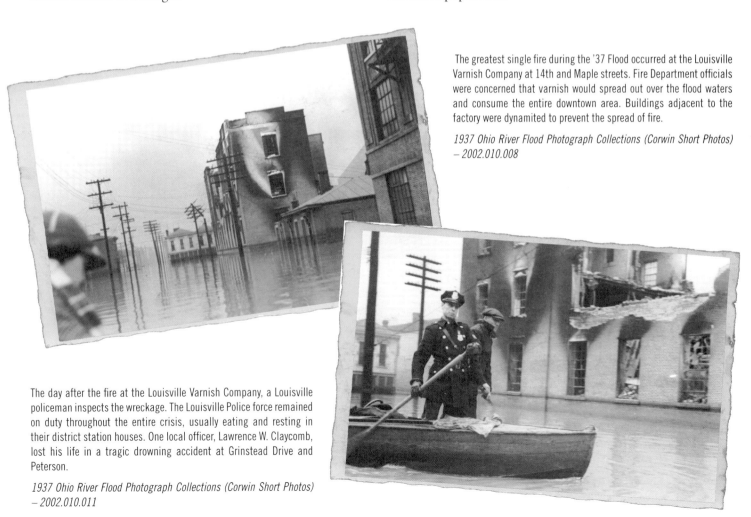

The greatest single fire during the '37 Flood occurred at the Louisville Varnish Company at 14th and Maple streets. Fire Department officials were concerned that varnish would spread out over the flood waters and consume the entire downtown area. Buildings adjacent to the factory were dynamited to prevent the spread of fire.

1937 Ohio River Flood Photograph Collections (Corwin Short Photos) – 2002.010.008

The day after the fire at the Louisville Varnish Company, a Louisville policeman inspects the wreckage. The Louisville Police force remained on duty throughout the entire crisis, usually eating and resting in their district station houses. One local officer, Lawrence W. Claycomb, lost his life in a tragic drowning accident at Grinstead Drive and Peterson.

1937 Ohio River Flood Photograph Collections (Corwin Short Photos) – 2002.010.011

Bardstown Road: The New Fourth Avenue

The extent of the disruption to Louisville's East End is obvious in this dramatic aerial photo. The Big Four Bridge is shown crossing the Ohio River on the left side, while the center of the photo shows the swollen current of Beargrass Creek separating downtown Louisville from the Highlands. The un–developed landscape located in the lower right side is Cave Hill Cemetery at the eastern terminus of Broadway.

1937 Ohio River Flood Photograph Collections – 1986.62.1

January 28–31, 1937

After the crest had been reached, conditions slowly began to improve. Following January 27, four days of little or no rain allowed some utilities to begin restoring services. On January 28, the Highlands received additional current, allowing more power for lighting. The next day, Crescent Hill began receiving additional power from Kentucky Utilities. Also, the L&N Railroad was able to begin a shuttle service between Crescent Hill and downtown to ease transportation problems. By January 31, the daily water ration was increased to three hours a day.

It was during this period that for one week, Bardstown Road replaced Fourth Street as the busiest avenue in Louisville. Thousands of people jammed sidewalks from Baxter Avenue to the Douglass Loop, and West End residents bumped into so many friends and associates they thought they were still in Parkland or Shawnee. Traffic continually moved materials, equipment and refugees to–and–from relief stations.

The Musical Arts Building became known as "Jerry Diggins' Hospital" providing first aid, typhoid injections and medical assistance. Improvised counters appeared on sidewalks in the Highlands that distributed provisions, manned information bureaus and filed missing persons' reports. On side streets like Alfresco and Speed Avenue, emergency comfort stations

– outhouses – were set up over manholes feeding directly into the city's sewers.

One old–timer believed the previous record–setting flood of 1884 was a worse disaster than the '37 Flood. He observed that 50 years before there were no Highlands or Crescent Hill neighborhoods with their large schools and churches providing refuge.

Few relief stations were as well–situated as K.M.I., the Kentucky Military Institute, in Lyndon. The large school was unoccupied because students were attending their winter session in Florida. Their bedding, kitchen supplies, and cooking tools were all in Florida with the students. After being given permission to use the property, volunteers began to scavenge and locate mattresses, bedding, fresh sources of drinking water and a kitchen. Two ex–servicemen, one from the Army and the other from the Marine Corps, took charge of preparing meals for the steady stream of hungry incoming refugees and staff.

Medical and hospital supplies were brought in from the recently–evacuated Jewish Hospital in Louisville. Volunteers formed themselves into committees to provide security, transportation, medical services and all other duties required by a small town. Even a sign painter was located to design directional and informational posters. The volunteers were so

Living with Strangers

Thousands of Louisville families welcomed complete strangers into their homes during the Flood crisis. Becoming a refugee in your own home town was stressful, but being a host family also had its challenges. Louisvillian Reba Doutrick recalls her childhood memories of sharing her family home with strangers.

"We lived in South Louisville, off Taylor Boulevard, just a few blocks north of the entrance of Iroquois Park. The flood waters stopped at Gahlinger's Hill, near Taylor and Bicknell.

A family of refugees came to stay with us. I don't know how they got there. There were two small children, one of whom was less than a year old. We had a cow in the back yard shed, so all of us had fresh milk to drink. There were four children in our family, and our house was rather small. I had the distinct impression that our guests were unfriendly. Looking back at it now, I'm sure they were worried about their uncertain future, and didn't like being uprooted and forced to live with strangers. Then, I just wanted to play with the baby, and was coldly rebuffed."

Refugees were loaded into, and sometimes on the roof of, emergency trains sent to communities in six states. A train yard, usually used to transport livestock, was located near the Bourbon Stock Yards near the confluence of the three branches of Beargrass Creek.

1937 Ohio River Flood Photograph Collections (Corwin Short Photos) – 2002.010.064

dedicated they felt ashamed when they fell asleep and apologized to co–workers when they awoke.

The relief station at K.M.I. housed 500 desperate refugees. There were no casualties and the visitors, both volunteers and refugees, left the school in better condition than when they arrived.

By the end of January, limited bus service was reinstituted, with many routes being closed by street cave–ins. Temporary bridges were built, pavement was replaced by wooden blocks, and people gradually regained the ability to commute. Automobile drivers were warned not to drive through flood waters as there was no sure knowledge a street still existed under them. Motorists were told to avoid the potholes and cave–ins at 19th and Duncan, Main between 15th and 16th, 17th and Magazine, 12th between Jefferson and Market, Woodland between 25th and 26th, First between College and Breckinridge, Kentucky from First to Fourth streets, St. Catherine at Shelby and Logan and Third at Whitney.

At the outset of the crisis, looting was anticipated and orders were given to police and Army personnel that they were to "shoot to kill." Despite this stern and frequently communicated policy, no one was shot and very few arrested. Liquor stores were favorite targets of looters. On January 29, three alleged thieves were arrested with a boatload of liquor and blankets. Mike Sullivan, Amos Willis and James Worden were accused of storehouse breaking and banding together to commit a felony. The violators were pressed into relief work and instructed to return to the jail after the flood was over.

Temporary privies were erected on side streets in the Highlands neighborhood. This outhouse, located at Alfresco Place and Bardstown Road, provided relief to refugees passing through the neighborhood. To provide sanitation facilities, man–hole covers were removed from the streets and simple sheds were constructed to provide a little privacy for grateful citizens. Men's and Women's outhouses were assembled, and clearly marked to be gender–specific.

1937 Ohio River Flood Photograph Collections – 1986.56.1

A group of refugees watch in the Highlands for relatives or loved ones from whom they were separated in the mad rush from the flooded districts of the city.

Mayor's Scrapbook – page 48-B

Breaking and Entering with Style

Two enterprising young Portland men recognized opportunity when they saw it. While heading home past the corner of 26th Street and Portland Avenue in a small motorboat, brothers Jack and Tom Byrne passed a darkened liquor store with large glass windows flanking the door. The windows were semi–submerged in the muddy brown water. Throwing a tarp over their heads, the Byrne brothers powered through the left side window and into the inviting store. Inventory still sat on high shelves behind the counter. After availing themselves of some merchant's wares, they swiveled their boat and prepared to exit. Instead of going out their original entrance, they again donned the tarpaulin and smashed through the remaining window.

Luckert's Drug Store, located at 934 West Market, shows the aftermath of breaking–and–entering burglary during the crisis. Liquor stores, pharmacies and groceries were prime targets for break–ins, with alcohol and cigarettes being common targets for thieves. Authorized officials also broke into stores to gather supplies that were distributed for relief purposes, but they left behind receipts.

R.G. Potter Collection – 2309

Eventually, reports surfaced of over 750 small businesses that were victims of looting. Grocery and drug stores were hard hit, with merchants claiming losses exceeding $1,000,000. These reports did not account for all the official confiscations made by police and National Guardsmen. On many occasions, officials would clean out an inventory and leave a receipt, sometimes written in pencil on the wall, to facilitate reimbursement.

Reports of deaths were becoming more common. Rumors swept the town, often aided by erroneous press reports. An out–of–town Associated Press reporter sent over the wire that "900 bodies were seen floating," and unburied bodies were being cremated or hurried into mass graves.

The actual number of drowning victims was small, only six confirmed deaths during the entire crisis in Louisville. A white man in overalls was reported drowned near Taylor Boulevard, while an African–American was found at Fifth and Breckinridge and another in the 600 block of South 34th Street. At one point, 46 corpses were reported at Barret's Funeral Home on Bardstown Road.

To prevent the spread of disease the City ordered the quarantine of the entire West End on January 31. Twelve square miles, all of the area west of 18th and north of Algonquin Parkway, were closed to the public. This allowed building inspectors an opportunity to investigate unstable structures, and all persons returning to the area were required to show proof they had received their shots.

The National Guard and State Police maintained posts on every road leading into Louisville and only emergency vehicles with signed permits could enter. Evacuated refugees were not allowed to return to their homes until the Department of Health had conducted inspections, but those who had braved the flood in their second–floor residences were allowed to stay.

Many West End residents stayed in their homes, concerned with protecting their possessions, maintaining heat in their building, and keeping their families together. Dorothy and Fred Bell lived above the E. D. Whitehouse grocery at 3101 Portland Avenue. They were able to secure canned goods and other supplies from the store below, but heating their small apartment was a constant concern. Dot Bell's greatest problem was how to wash and dry diapers for her six–month–old son Russell. The problem was solved by going up into the store's attic and bringing down the grocer's antique furniture, which they broke up and burned in a small wood stove.

The extent of flooding in Louisville's West End was staggering. This aerial view, looking north from Cecil Avenue, shows the entrance of the old State Fair Grounds as a submerged white arch in the lower center of the photo. On January 31, 12 square miles of the West End were placed under quarantine to prevent the spread of disease, and to allow officials to inspect damaged structures.

Goodman-Paxton – Box 6 Item 306

Painful Shots Pay Dividends

Many Louisvillians, especially in the West End, waited out the Flood in upper–story apartments. Since electricity and water service was uncertain in every area of the city, many felt they were safer staying home. Food was often supplied by boat crews during their rounds of patrolling the flooded areas.

1937 Ohio River Flood Photograph Collections (Corwin Short Photos) – 2002.010.090

Public health was the foremost concern. Extreme conditions caused by the incessant rainfall, bitterly cold temperatures, immersions and the presence of communicable diseases signaled the potential for a true disaster. Dr. Hugh R. Leavell, the City of Louisville's Director of Health, led the fight to preserve health and resist epidemics. He instructed citizens to boil their water and add a drop of iodine to every gallon.

Dr. Leavell also demanded that every person over the age of two receive inoculations of typhoid serum. The recommended dosage was a series of three shots, one every five days. Everyone who received the shots, more than 175,000 Louisvillians, reported how painful and numb their arms remained after their injections. Even after a passage of 70 years, when an aging flood veteran is asked about the shots, his first reaction is to reach up and protect his left upper arm.

Shots were given everywhere, from Library basements to church sanctuaries. They were routinely administered in the rescue boats and often on roof–tops while waiting to board a boat. During the crisis, hypodermic needles were used repeatedly until they became too dull for comfort.

Two essential public figures, Mayor Neville Miller (center) and Dr. Hugh R. Leavell (right), Louisville's Director of Health, are shown in a publicity photo taken shortly before the flood with an unknown veterinarian and dog. Leavell's brilliant administration during the Flood was credited with saving thousands of lives through his aggressive campaign to provide typhoid inoculations. Shortly after the Flood, Dr. Leavell was named Dean of the Harvard University School of Public Health, and his advocacy of primary prevention became a cornerstone of American public health policy.

Herald Post – 2485

Valuable typhoid serum was delivered to the city from Philadelphia in a private airplane. When the pilot landed, he hurriedly commented, "It's a gift to the Mayor of Louisville from the Mayor of Philadelphia." More typhoid anti–toxin serum was rushed to the city from Boston and a Coast Guard facility in New Jersey. Before the crisis was over, an estimated 80 gallons of serum had been shipped to Kentucky.

Free vaccine was given out at stations scattered throughout the community: the Portland Branch Library and Highland Park Center, Crittenden Drive and Hiawatha; fire stations at 221 S. Hancock, 1617 W. Main, 1509 S. Sixth, 1024 Logan, Frankfort and Pope; and Churchill Downs. An isolation and contagion hospital was established in the Crescent Hill Christian Church, but it was closed on February 4 for lack of patients needing its care.

City Hospital, located at Preston and Chestnut streets, saw water at its front door. The wide front steps leading up from the sidewalk provided an ideal landing for small boats delivering some patients, and taking others to the Pontoon Bridge for evacuation. An impromptu sign, made with red paint on a bed sheet, proclaimed "Hospital Boat Landing."

The City Hospital had a new Annex scheduled to be available in six weeks, but its formal opening could not wait. Electricians feverously finished installing lighting fixtures while medical professionals prepared to begin treating the expected crowds of patients. The odor of new paint mingled with medicinal smells and unwashed bodies. Within days, J. B. Bushemeyer, superintendent of the City Hospital, said there were 862 cases of all types being treated in his hospital alone.

The administration of the City Hospital sped up other things as well. The entire senior medical school class of the University of Louisville, scheduled to graduate in June, went immediately to work as regular physicians. Junior class members were detailed to give anti–toxin injections at relief stations.

The hospital maintained a steady supply of distilled water,

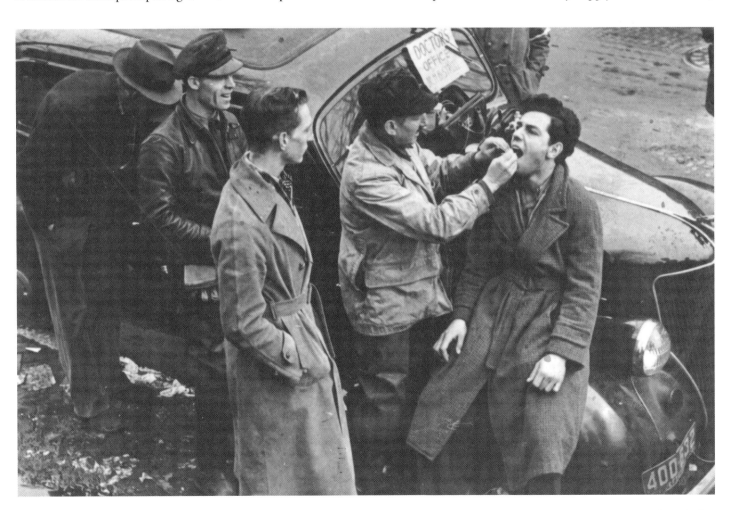

An improvised doctor's office on a car fender provided a temporary medical treatment center at Relief Station B–21, located at First and Breckinridge streets. The station's public health efforts were directed by Dr. H. B. Strull. During the crisis, tens of thousands of refugees received emergency treatment in the hastily–prepared relief stations.

R.G. Potter Collection – 6004

thanks to the Frank Fehr Brewing Company and Seagram Distillery, which used their own trucks to deliver the free and sanitary water. Louisville produce dealers and importers helped by donating 1,500 quarts of fresh strawberries and large quantities of other perishable fruits and vegetables.

In Crescent Hill, an improvised hospital clinic began to serve thousands of patients. Charles Tachau had organized an emergency hospital in the Barret Junior High School to treat refugees pouring from the east end of the Pontoon Bridge. Dr. J. Murray Kinsman served as chief of staff to the 21 volunteer doctors and 18 nurses, who manned the clinic in its early days. The doctors on call were: Drs. Kinsman, McKeithen, Joplin, Imes, Allen, Strickler, Richey,

Wilson, Knight, Harman, Howard, Goldsborough, Leigh, Moore, Karraker, Myer, Keifer, Pryor, Townes, Bass and Atherton. The nurses were Misses Dade, Quingley, Lindley, Beard, Bissing, Hagood, Sexton, Ford, Herr, Heine, Hicks, Taylor, Parker, Whitehurst, Barnes, Hardesty and Mary and Elizabeth Blandford.

On the last day of the fateful month of January 1937, the civilian doctors were replaced by a medical company from Company G, First Medical Regiment, Carlisle Barracks, Pennsylvania. Commanded by Capt. Alvin L. Gordy, the 98-man medical unit carried its own equipment, medical supplies, and provided enough bed capacity to treat 250 patients. They brought with them 1,200 Army blankets and enough food to supply themselves for ten days.

The front steps of Louisville City Hospital served as a boat landing dock for sick and injured people during the Flood. The City Hospital, located at Preston and Chestnut streets, was the primary center for local healthcare, with over 800 patients being treated during the height of the crisis. The Medical School's entire senior class were declared doctors three months prior to their scheduled graduation, and the newly-accredited physicians were pressed into emergency service.

1937 Ohio River Flood Photograph Collections – 1986.38B.01

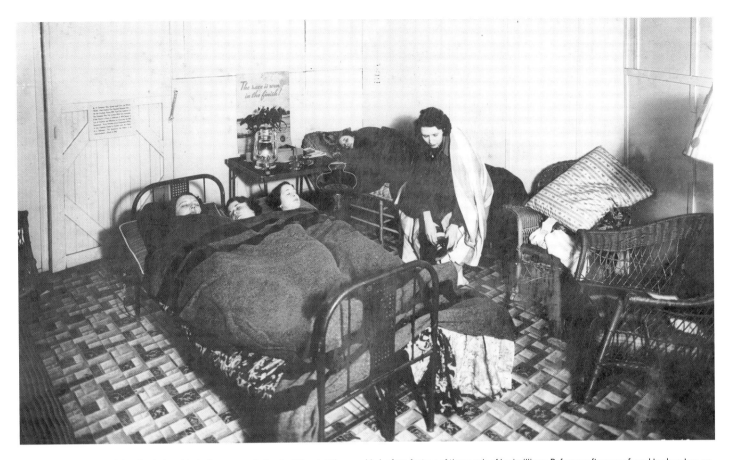

Relief centers were crowded, unheated, and lacked proper sanitation facilities, but they provided refuge for tens of thousands of Louisvillians. Refugees often were forced to sleep two—or—three to a bed, and such crowding was a breeding ground for communicable diseases. Despite such dire conditions, only 90 deaths in Louisville were directly attributed to the Flood.

1937 Ohio River Flood Photograph Collections – 1986.62.2

Initially, health officials took a very pessimistic view of the emerging crisis. They predicted 15,000 cases of pneumonia, especially among the exhausted relief workers. A typhoid epidemic was considered inevitable and scarlet fever had already broken out among refugees in the Lowe's Theatre (now Louisville Palace). Nine undertakers were deputized by coroner Dr. John M. Kearney.

When talking to Flood veterans, many people volunteer their firmly–held opinion that "nobody died during the Flood." This statement is always made with a feeling of pride and accomplishment. Local media deliberately downplayed reports of deaths, and news of deaths were often delayed. Despite the persistent myth of public safety, in reality 90 deaths could be directly attributed to the Great Flood in Louisville. Statistics provided by the City Health Service give the following list of fatalities:

- 6 drownings
- 2 asphyxiations
- 10 deaths due to exposure
- one death due to dysentery
- 15 burn and explosion victims
- 28 fatalities caused by pneumonia (in excess of the average)
- 28 cases of heart attacks (in excess of the average)

One of the great wonders of the 1937 Flood is not that people died, it is that many more did not. For months afterwards, many local deaths could be directly attributed to the stress of the Flood. Several well–known public officials died within weeks of the crisis. Professor George Tilden Ragsdale was the founder and superintendent of the Louisville Police Academy, and for 22 years a member of the faculty of Louisville Male High School. By February 2, he had worked himself to death. Mayor Miller stated "the professor's death undoubtedly can be traced to his incessant labor during the flood emergency. He was a loveable and remarkable man."

Professor George T. Ragsdall taught school at Louisville Male High for decades and was also the founder of the Louisville Police Academy. His dedication to public service was cited by Mayor Miller as the cause of his death. Professor Ragsdall was one of several volunteer supervisors who died from overwork, pneumonia or exhaustion.

Herald-Post – 1994.18.3074

In two weeks a better known community leader died of pneumonia. "General" Percy Haly had been an important political figure in Kentucky since the death of his political mentor, the assassinated governor, William Goebel. Appointed Deputy Provost Marshal, Haly used his savvy, political know–how and sheer determination to cut red tape and solve problems. During his rare breaks for sleep, the 65 year old Haly climbed up and down 13 flights of stairs to his heatless room in the Brown Hotel.

While some left this world during the Great Flood, others entered. By late January, City Hospital officials announced that 54 babies had been born and 20 expectant mothers were in the hospital. One baby was born in a rescue truck en route from Crescent Hill to Greensburg, Indiana, and another on a train heading out of town. An infant declared to be "Louisville's highest–born baby" was delivered on the 16th floor of the Kentucky Hotel.

The distinction of being probably the only baby ever born in the U.S. Marine Hospital belongs to Janet Marine Cook Meredith. When her mother went into labor, her father rushed from his job at the Portland Canal and tried to locate medical help. They went to the old United States Marine Hospital on High Street, a medical facility that had for the previous 85 years treated sick and injured Ohio River boatmen, rugged Coast Guard surfmen and recuperating World War I veterans. The Marine Hospital was not the kind of facility that offered a maternity ward.

While the boilers that provided heat to the new Louisville Memorial Hospital next door were flooded, the coal fireplaces in the old boatman's hospital worked very well. Janet Marine Cook was born on January 28, the day after the flood crest, and received her middle name as a reminder.

"Be our dove, and tell us what you've seen when you return."

The community pulled together and found answers to challenges never before faced. Excerpts from a *Courier–Journal* story tell how the flood converted the Tourist Lawn Hotel, 1241 South Third Street, into a place of refuge. The remembrance was written by Virginia Marquette Shirley, an assistant at the Louisville Free Public Library, whose father was proprietor of the hotel.

Lame, Halt, Blind, Black, White Housed at Third St. Island Hotel

Into our home, which seemed a safe haven in the beginning, began to come those who were forced to seek higher ground. There were about a dozen living in the home to begin with, and we gladly made room for unfortunates. Overnight our numbers grew rapidly.

Those who received (the refugees) gave hot food, comfort and courage. Our numbers grew to forty–eight persons, including two infants, three children, two Negroes and a miscellaneous assemblage of individuals shrieking with nerves, and fears, and fatigue.

As the radio calls grew more frantic, and water reports came closer to our home, fear grew in our house and the realization that we must all work desperately to save our minds in order to save our bodies.

The second day brought a rise of four feet to our street. We were an island.

The corner grocery flooded. The neighborhood druggist worked to save his stock. The grocer said, "Take what you can save." The druggist moved in with his store.

Confusion in our hearts beat hard against the radio voices of disaster and horrors. The water had reached our furnace in the basement. No heat, except a few gas grates and a blessing of a stove. The water grew and threatened the staunch gas meter. The men worked frantically to stop the basement flood and did just in time. Women worked hard to prepare water and save the perishable foods in our supplies….The sleet and snow came.

Organization. That was our salvation. We all contributed our concentrated efforts on the immediate problem at hand. We established a commissary, a water committee, a diplomatic committee, and a 24 hour guard. Everyone began to work and the work gave us sanity…We hoped, we prayed, we sang, to beat down the fear of water, fire, disease, madness. …Our men miraculously acquired boats, boots, and a renewed nerve as the rain stopped. Our island became a small community of local gossip, neighborly errands.

In the darkness a man was fished from the river and warmed and dressed. Around the one candle faces drawn and tired, hands working against time.

In the street a blind man struggled,

Employees at a local bank gathered around a temporary wood–burning stove to seek warmth. Financial institutions worked hard to keep their doors open and provide at least minimal services to the public. Cashing checks or money orders was limited, but was a necessity in the days prior to credit cards or ATM machines.

1937 Ohio River Flood Photograph Collections – 1986.47.2

waist–deep along the pavement, tapping and waving his cane. It became advisable to remove an old lady and a baby to safer ground. In a staunch boat, with rain pelting our bodies, the lady, the baby, and I were taken away.

"Be our dove," they called to me, "and tell us what you've seen when you return."

We were taken along familiar, yet strange, streets. Our street, under the white moon of the night before, had appeared a vague, fantastic fairyland. Snow–covered, the tall, old houses reflected in the water, under the moon–light, had assumed the beauteous dignity of a Venetian canal. It had a magic, ethereal look. But in the day, the abandoned homes, submerged cars, floating debris, unhappy, discouraged faces haunting windows, looted, broken shops were a ghastly reality.

A relief car rushed me through dreary streets to the Highlands. At the Loop, all was activity, a center of charity. More organization and desperate fight to carry on. Hot meals cooked by socialites; clothes given by business men; nurses, doctors, engineers, electricians, policemen, food, vehicles. One felt the spirit of it all. All doors in the Highlands, homes imposing or humble, were open. All hearts were open too.

Bread lines beginning everywhere and going around endless corners, black and white huddled against walls together. On and on, through markets empty of produce and jammed with people. Stinking holes, water pumps madly chugging, fire–trucks clanging, garbage rotting, policemen screaming oaths. Vistas through cross–streets to the churning river.

When day came, armed with a pass, much confidence and supplies, I returned to the sergeant.

"The City Hospital," said the Sergeant. "I can get a high truck there."

The back entrance was high and dry, but the front door had deep water. Going to the office for a permit, we passed through crowded corridors, lined with emergency cots, holding pale, disinterested bodies.

Doctors and nurses carried on despite their own soiled linen and smelly bodies, with mouths closed grimly against the bemingled odors of steamy hallways.

At the boat landing, in the deeper water, were floaters of every type from hand–made scows and rafts to outboards and canoes. Even a South American dugout, with a carved figure–head.

"The Army and the police are not exactly happy together," explained my protector. "But we get along."

We plied the streets. Lifted groceries onto a porch where a wane mother exclaimed with relief. Dropped supplies in an alley refuge.

Children clasped their bread loaves in their arms lovingly and hugged the cereal box as though it was a doll.

At last, just twenty–four hours afterward, I reached home, when under normal times the journey would have been made in ten minutes. I was, indeed, the dove returning to the Ark, with an armful of *Courier–Journals* to show the marooned refugees.

Passes were required for persons wishing to return to flooded areas of town. Everyone had to show proof of receiving their inoculations and needed a valid reason for leaving safety. In rented offices in the Louisville Hotel, National Guard and State Health officials issued passes and maintained records of persons reported missing.

Caufield and Shook Collection – 149607

Police and other officials used hotel beds as desks during the Flood crisis. A woman (on right) is shown being interviewed, probably while filing a missing persons report. From temporary offices like these, health officials coordinated efforts to inspect food and drug dispensaries, and regulated public health and sanitation measures.

Caufield and Shook Collection – 149609

Normally a busy business address, the corner of Sixth Street looking south from Main, presents an ethereal image as the calm waters resemble a canal in downtown Louisville.

Caufield and Shook Collection – 149496

"...it was slow soaking and settling slime which wrought ruin"

February 1–22, 1937

By February 1, the descending flood stage was standing at 52.6 feet, still 24.5 feet above normal flood stage. Although a crisis remained, the city was slowly beginning to get back on its feet. The Cardinal Hill reservoir was tapped to provide the first water service to South Louisville, Beechmont and Highland Park. City bus lines were opened on Walnut, Market and Fourth streets.

On February 2, the boilers were fired at the Riverside Pumping Station and the city's water ration was increased. The Oak Street and Crescent Hill bus lines began to operate and two square miles of the West End were freed from quarantine restrictions.

By February 3, the city was receiving water service from 8 a.m. until 5 p.m., and telephone service was restored to the Shawnee exchange. On February 4, a second pump was started at the Riverside water plant and the city resumed 24–hour water service. Also on that day, the first electrical service was fed to the downtown area.

The Flood's crest is easily–recognizable in this interior photo of an unidentified house. Standing water has stripped the wallpaper, warped the floor–boards and shattered furniture. Virtually all middle–class West End homes had pianos ruined by the floodwaters. After the crisis, scavengers were seen stripping the ivory off thousands of waterlogged keyboards.

Caufield and Shook Collection – 149371

One thinks of flood as a violent force, tornado–like in lateral pressure, sweeping all before it. Not so in backwater, or sluggish currents slowed down by walls and embankments.

As in Paducah, under water for 15 days or more, it was slow soaking and settling slime which wrought ruin. Walls and foundations crumbled; in shop windows light objects of merchandise floated foolishly about on top of the water. Candy in showcases turned to glucose masses streaked with color. In a drugstore rows of muddy bottles stood on shelves, their labels soaked off, and a newsstand rack was a mass of sodden, swollen pulp.

In homes, saturated mattresses and upholstery bloated to twice normal size; wallpaper peeled; rugs were thick with slime and mud: pianos and cheap, glued chairs and tables literally fell to pieces.

National Geographic, 1937

By February 5, all restrictions were removed from the West End and residents were allowed to return to their homes to begin the work of cleanup. The lifelong citizens of Louisville's most flood–prone neighborhoods – Portland, Shippingport and the Point – then discovered they had one advantage over their traditionally more dry–shod neighbors. These flood veterans knew the important practice of being in the house as the waters began to recede. By being present they were able to sweep and shovel water and mud out, even while the house began to dry. This helped preserve wooden floors and plaster walls, and greatly simplified the tedious process of cleanup.

Elinor and Joe

Despite the absolute disruption to their lives, Louisvillians began to plan their futures. Joe Maloney, a supervisor with Reynold's Metals, was hurriedly sent to New York when the company's West End plant was closed by the flood. His young wife, the former Elinor Fromang, and their one–year–old son, Joe, Jr., remained in Louisville. Their letters during the crisis provide insight into the frustration caused by slow communications and physical separation. Despite evacuating her Parkland home and the sure certainty that almost all possessions were lost, Elinor Maloney spent her time preparing for her family's future. She made plans on where to move and how to restore a semblance of normalcy to domestic life. She had high hopes for her new nest, *"The way I plan it our place should be real cute."*

At the beginning of the flood crisis, Joe Maloney was sent by his employer out-of-town to their plant in New York. He and his young wife, Elinor Fromang Maloney, maintained a lively correspondence during the Flood. Most of Elinor's insightful letters deal with the well-being of their one-year-old son Joe, Jr. and their family's living conditions. Elinor Maloney's optimistic plans for domestic security were illustrative of Louisvillians' determination to return to normalcy, and to make their futures brighter.

Photo collection of Mike Maloney

Friday, February 5, '37

Dearest Joe,
I got my last shot several hours ago and I'm afraid it's going to give me trouble. My arm feels like a dead weight.
There is a big fire in town tonite. Has been burning since about 2:30 p.m. at Floyd and Market as the result of a gas explosion. It is the southwest corner, I think, a drug store and A&P and other stores and flats.
My arm hurts so I can hardly think to write. I got the shot over at the fire house and they put it right in that big muscle that goes along the side of one's arm - that is why it pains so I guess.

February 12, 1937

Dearest Joe,
At the risk of sounding monotonous I'm telling you again how much I miss you, my sweetheart, especially in the evenings and at night. I had been used to not having you during the day but "oh these lonesome nights."
I got your Valentine today my darling. It was so sweet. That word always you underscored is a nice word isn't it? It makes this time while we are separated not seem so long compared to the time we'll be together.
Your mama said you were smart getting out of all that work and mess down home. She said tell you she said so. I'm glad you're out of it. I get a really sick headache each time I go down. Will have to close so Goodnight my love.

Elinor

p.s. We got lights yesterday at 5:00 p.m.
Ginny and Austin said, Don't take any wooden nickels.

February 14, 1937

Dearest Joe,

Tomorrow I'm going down and pack our dishes and the rest of what clothes are there and stack whatever is salvageable for Austin or Francis to get tomorrow or next day. Then after those things are taken out I can forget about that place down there. Our radiant heater seems o.k. Your mother is looking for rooms but hasn't found any as yet. They couldn't live down there anyway till the place is practically made over. The floors have all buckled, doors warped, paper ruined, plaster stinks etc. I can look at that awful place and things look so familiar and yet so strange that it all seems like a nightmare.

---

2 18 1937

Dearest Elinor and Baby Joe,

I got a letter from Mother yesterday and she said she was looking at some rooms down on Hemlock and the way she talks she wants to live with us as we did before but I am going to write and tell her that we are going to try to get us some rooms ourselves for I think it would be better for all of us. I hope you have found a couple of nice rooms by now so we can go into them when I get back for I don't want to stay at any ones house if I can help it. So Honey, if you have found the rooms you should use your own judgment about getting the furniture. But as I said before get something new for we will have to use it for a long time.

Joe

February 20, 1937

Darling,

I sent our rug to the cleaner. It will cost $3.25. They said it might not be back for 5 or 6 weeks though as they had over 400 rugs to clean. The flood certainly has made some businesses boom.

The baby's toys are not ruined. You don't have to bring me a present, but since you want to what about an umbrella. I could keep that a long time or a pair of house slippers (6 ½) or some kind of lamp, book ends or clock or something for our house. (It seems too good to be true that we'll have a home of our own at last - at least it seems good to me.)

I hardly know what you could get for our dolly. (Maybe a case of Coca-Cola's). He needs a bank.

Honey, get our mothers some little notion, a couple of towels or a pretty bowl, or some hankies or something. Writing paper is another nice thing.

A Charlie Fogle about 50 was killed in that fire at the varnish company. I wonder if he was related to Jake? The man downstairs works for Molls and was the one who found his body, burnt to a crisp, he said. Jake's brother works there don't he?

I've ordered us a kitchen linoleum to be delivered when we get a place. I'm making my mind up what other pieces to get. The way I plan it our place should be real cute. I'm going house hunting again tomorrow, that is if there is time before or after your parents come.

Lots of streets are sinking due to sewer cave ins. 4th between Liberty and Walnut is one place that is blocked off.

That's going to be a fine birthday isn't it sweetheart. I hope you can make it. It will be the fourth we've known together. Do you realize that? The first one you were begging me to kiss you (remember?). But this one you'll be begging me to stop. But I warn you it will do you no good. I love you so much my darling - you're on my mind, down beneath what ever I may be doing or saying, all the time. I don't remember how I felt before I had you to love, it seems like you must have always been there in my heart, as you will be forever.

Darling there isn't anything of interest to write and as it is nearly twelve, I'd better close and get some sleep.

With all our love,
Elinor and little you.

P.S. The other day out at Lorene's Joe was just in raptures over a grey felt hat he thought was yours - and guess what - he's learned to whistle. Oh, I didn't mention the money you sent - Thanks Honey.

Dearest Joe,

February 24, 1937

Darling, there are two rooms on Frankfort Avenue across from the Blind School that I think I can get Saturday. They are furnished and rent for 4 dollars a week. I have been looking several times since you wrote me not to come up there but it has been so cold to take Joseph and he is such a load to carry that I haven't been able to look very far or thoroughly.

So sweetheart if we can get those rooms for a few weeks we can be together there until we find something else. They are real nice rooms in a two story brick. There will be some unfurnished ones for rent in the same house the 13th of next month and we could take them then if you wanted to or after we get the car fixed up we can look more in other neighborhoods.

I would have liked to have our own things when you come back. But I just haven't had a chance to get things as I want them. I want our linoleum varnished and a lot of things like that done before we start living in our own love nest. So we can find our place, move our furniture in etc. while we are staying in those rooms.

They're reasonable I think. I can make draperies, wash and stretch our curtains while we live over there. Too, our rug won't be back for another month and I couldn't fix us a very pretty bedroom without it.

Disaster at the A&P

The most devastating accident during the crisis was an explosion on the southwest corner of Floyd and Market streets on February 5, 1937. A large commercial building housing an A&P grocery, Eckerle Drug Store, a jeweler and a tire company, blew apart and burned following a natural gas leak. Ten deaths were caused by the accident, which killed shop–owners and residents of apartments located above the stores.

Postcard Collection – 1981.43.30

The big fire described by Elinor Maloney occurred on February 5. The single deadliest event during the Flood was a gas explosion and fire that killed 10 people in a three–story building on the corner of Floyd and Market. On the street level, the building housed the Eckerle Drug Store, a jewelry shop, the Breckinridge Brothers Tire Company and an A&P grocery. The top two floors were divided into 15 apartments.

Men, women and children were seen leaping from second–story windows when rescuers arrived. A total of 125 WPA workers, under the direction of Public Works engineer E. F. Schimpeler, were summoned from Crescent Hill and worked frantically to free those trapped in the rubble.

Jewelry store operator Israel Monfried reported, "All I know is that the walls reached out and hit me." The manager of the tire store, Mohler Breckinridge was trapped under a girder and frantic efforts were made at rescue. He died when rescue crews were withdrawn when the building began collapsing around them. Mrs. Mary Smith was in shock when taken to City Hospital to have her burns and bruises treated. "I lost my pocketbook, but I still have my key which isn't much good now I guess."

Two victims of the explosion and fire were Mrs. Jenette Adcock and her five–year old son, Roy. They were caught inside the A&P store and were unable to escape. Their father and grandfather was a firefighter, Jacob Fitch, who had helped battle the blaze with no idea his family was among the victims.

After 18 days above flood stage, on Sunday, February 7, the Ohio River finally descended to its normal flood stage of 28 feet. On that day electrical power was restored to all areas, including the West and South Ends. Churches were allowed to reopen that Sunday and the serious work of cleanup and assessment had begun.

Local architects were appointed to inspect houses and commercial buildings to check for structural damage. Thirty–five buildings in the city were declared unsafe and condemned. By February 9, streets were being cleaned, debris from the high water and uncollected garbage was picked up in the non–flooded areas of town. Many streets were littered with abandoned boats, left high–and–dry after the waters had retreated. The city of Cleveland sent three street flushers to add to Louisville's four. The tedious work of removing silt, garbage, shattered houses and oil slicks had begun.

LG&E estimated that 40,000 electric meters and 35,000 gas meters required removal and cleaning. The Welfare Department closed the refugee center in the County Armory that had served

Workers in a local distillery smashed thousands of glass whiskey bottles contaminated during the Flood. Proper disposal of ruined food, beverage and medicinal products required the efforts of thousands of temporary workers. Federal assistance to hire local workers had a beneficial impact on a city just emerging from the Great Depression and the enormous expenses of the 1937 Flood.

Caufield and Shook Collection –153103

75,000 people during the crisis.

One of the surest signs that life was returning to normal occurred on February 12, when the local high school basketball schedule was resumed. By February 22, 43 public schools reopened. Two high schools, Shawnee and Dunbar, remained closed the remainder of the school year and major re–adjustments were needed to accommodate those students in other schools. Four elementary schools remained closed for the year.

Two hundred and fifty of the city's 300 churches had been affected by the flooding, but most were able to reopen immediately. The hardest hit was Portland's Church of Our Lady (Notre Dame du Port) on Rudd Avenue and 35th Street.

No area of the city suffered more devastating impact than Portland's Rudd Avenue. The church is located three blocks south of the old Portland Wharf, which rested more than 33 feet underwater. Opposite the Church of Our Lady was the former Cedar Grove Academy, a private Catholic girl's finishing school founded in 1842. In 1925, after the school became Loretto High School and moved to Broadway, the grounds became known as "Cedar Grove Beautiful." Architect Otto Mock's stylized real estate development became one of the isolated elevated islands that dotted the West End.

Caufield and Shook Collection – 164420

The old French church had 22 feet of water standing in the building and the entire sanctuary floor collapsed into the basement. The hand–carved statue of Our Lady, imported from France in the 19th century, remained just above the water level on the high altar. Portland tradition tells that two wooden statues on the side altars floated around and repositioned themselves on their opposite altars. Notre Dame du Port did not reopen for another nine months.

To speed cleanup, City Division of Transportation dump truck drivers were instructed to drop their loads of debris directly into the Ohio River. Trucks drove to the middle of the Louisville Municipal Bridge (today's George Rogers Clark Memorial Bridge) and emptied their refuse over the guard rail.

R.G. Potter Collection – 3757

"...the most pitiful sight I had ever beheld."

The first place I went to see was my grandmother's house at 32nd and Rudd Avenue which is located about two squares from the river. When I saw her house, I knew that was the most pitiful sight I had ever beheld. Some of her furniture was out in the front yard and some in the back yard. There was even some hanging out of the upstairs window. Every piece of furniture that was picked up fell into a million pieces. Not one piece was saved. When the water went down, Grandmother's two sheds went down also. She even had one of the neighbor's houses leaning against hers. My girl friend, who lives a few doors from Grandmother, has a big tree on top of her house, and her shed was turned upside down in someone else's yard. The further down I went on Rudd the more pathetic the scenes became.

Alice Bonkofsky
Shawnee High School student

Water–soaked car seats and other materials were discarded in a make–shift dump behind the Ford Motor Company Plant on Southwestern Parkway. Cars caught in the factory when buildings were covered in flood waters were valuable company assets, and Ford ordered them restored. Fabrics were removed and disposed of, and car bodies and engines were carefully steam–cleaned, repainted and sold as new.

Caufield and Shook Collection – 149466

Louisville's refugees had been scattered over a six–state area and they were slowly returning home. Gasoline sales were opened to the public and travel was again becoming possible. Large city dumps and landfills were created to receive ruined furniture and supplies. Fifteen local dispensaries gave out chloride of lime, totaling more than two rail carloads, to aid in sanitization.

Over 700 tons of foodstuffs were destroyed by the flood waters. The dumps were guarded to prevent looting of the contaminated food. Thousands of pianos, once a fixture of nearly every middle–class home, were discarded and scavengers were seen stripping the ivory from the keyboards. One industrious Portland Irishman hired boys to cut up warped and ruined hardwood flooring into small straight strips, which he sold to contractors to make parquet floors.

The Mile Pond – a long low–lying area running between the Portland Canal and Northwestern Parkway – became the place of deposit for destroyed houses and their contents. Radio cabinets, dressers, mattresses, clothing and books were buried under the tons of silt being shoveled from the city's streets. In later years, this buried mountain of trash would evolve into Portland's Lannan Park.

WPA workers were busy in the West End pumping out basements of homes and businesses. The service was free, but residents were required to pay for the gasoline and oil used in the process.

Relief continued to arrive from the outside, but now it was possible for visiting volunteers to return to their homes. One of the grimmest tasks of the flood emergency was delayed until the waters had receded. Those who had died during the emergency had been embalmed and placed in vaults during the crisis. When the water receded and cemeteries had been cleared of debris, these victims were then buried.

Every building in the West End was inspected by architects to determine if any structural damage had occurred and if the building was safe for occupancy. The interior of an unidentified store shows the absolute destruction caused by flood waters. Flooded to the ceiling, inventory and store furniture were ruined. Within a few weeks, many local merchants were able to obtain loans to re–stock and repair their buildings.

R.G. Potter Collection – 2318.5

Basements in West End houses required pumping before furnaces could be lighted and drying the home's interior could begin. WPA workers provided free labor, but the cost of oil and gasoline to operate the pumps was the responsibility of the homeowner.

R.G. Potter Collection – 2312

"Sure it's bad, whether it's '84 or '37 it's always bad when your home gets flooded. The real trouble comes when she goes down, though, and leaves all the 'sentiment.'"

Old Hickory O'Neil
Shippingport shantyboatman

Aftermath

The economic impact of the Great Flood to Louisville and Jefferson County was staggering. It was estimated that the '37 Flood caused in excess of $52 million damage in Louisville alone (this represents more than $710 million in today's dollars). The public school systems suffered losses of over $500,000, and the Louisville Free Public Library lost an additional $184,750, nearly half of that figure in books alone. The Library's loss was greater than the sum of its annual operating budget, and monetary figures cannot include the loss of many irreplaceable books, records, manuscripts and works of art.

Only two of the ten buildings in the Louisville Free Public Library system escaped flooding. The Shawnee branch was completely submerged and needed a $25,000 renovation. Of all city departments, the library system was the hardest hit.

When the flood soaked the lower floors of the Library, thousands of books sat in the water and expanded. Swelling to three times their normal size, the books pushed through their shelves and splintered the wooden stacks. Librarian Harold F. Brigham called in an expert from Philadelphia, Dr. Charles W. Carroll, to supervise the work of restoration. Thirty thousand library books required expert drying, cleaning, disinfecting, ironing and rebinding. Dr. Carroll estimated it would take 60 persons working three months to accomplish the massive task. It was accomplished.

The Louisville Free Public Library system suffered enormous damage during the '37 Flood, with eight of ten facilities inundated. The Main Branch saw thousands of books, periodicals, maps and art work destroyed by the soaking waters. Library stacks were ruined as sodden books expanded and shattered the wooden shelves.

Louisville Free Public Library Collection – 1992.18.251

"Mummy Almost Drowned in Flood Will Dry Out Soon or Explode"

This unusual headline appeared in the March 30 edition of the *Courier–Journal.* Excerpts from Molly Clowes' byline story include the following interesting, but odd, highlights:

"Then–Hotep is irreverently known to most people merely as "the Library mummy." She arrived in Louisville some years ago, via the St. Louis Exposition, and until the flood she remained placidly enough the Library Museum's exhibit number one, furnishing thrills and shivers to countless visiting boys and girls.

Came the flood, and the strain was simply too much for Then–Hotep. She floated back and forth, fell face down in the mud, and lost her head. Her present visit to the Gas & Electric plant is admittedly a drastic experiment, according to Lucien Beckner, museum curator, who takes Then–Hotep's present dampness very much to heart. Her soaked rags will first be dried out for twenty–four hours at a gentle but steady heat. She will then be placed in the company's huge vacuum driers, from which she should emerge as near her original dessicated self as is possible in this world. If she doesn't, says Mr. Beckner, pessimistically, she'll explode in the vacuum, and that will be the end of Then–Hotep.

The body, lying out on the floor in an incongruous setting of turbines and generators was an object of considerable curiosity to engineers and workmen.

"It smells a little like old ham," murmured Mr. Beckner, sniffing a little and peering carefully into the muddy wrappings. "Curious…maybe they used wood smoke too…"

Hundreds of soldiers from Fort Knox were pressed into service to provide relief. In this souvenir post card, soldiers are shown bringing in bags of mail that had been undeliverable during the 18–day period of flooding. National organizations, like the Red Cross, WPA, CCC, U.S. Army and Coast Guard, added their might to the local volunteer effort and saved the Falls Cities and their citizens.

Postcard Collection – 1990.18.23

"...just one of those things that happen."

A car parked in front of Bybee Brothers Service Station, located at 315 West Oak Street, in today's Old Louisville neighborhood. Flood waters caused extraordinary damage to automobiles, ruining tires, fabric interiors and electrical systems. Local traffic patterns were disrupted by cave-ins and collapsed street pavement, making transportation especially difficult.

A Greater Louisville

(Ky. Irish American) 2-6-37

TO BE REBUILT BY THE UNITED
SPIRIT OF ALL ITS CITIZENS

Greatest Disaster In Fifty Years
Borne With Unflinching Courage

Mayor Miller, Man Of The Hour

Mayor's Scrapbook – Page 56-B

A steady rise in building projects and employment provided the stimulus for local economic growth. Building permits increased 52% over their total of the previous January. In commercial buildings, plumbing, elevators, furnaces, signs and boilers demanded replacement. It was estimated that 35,000 residences would require repairs estimated to average $300 each.

It is impossible to assign a dollar value to personal items destroyed by the '37 Flood. Countless family heirlooms perished in the muddy waters – as well as less significant items – photo albums, wedding gifts, souvenirs and children's favorite toys. It is equally impossible to calculate the grief caused by the loss of family pets – the dogs, cats and birds left behind when a family barely escaped with their own lives and the clothes on their backs.

The plight of Louisvillians, spread widely by radio, newspaper, magazines and newsreel accounts, became an international concern. Over $135,000 in personal donations were received along with cards, letters and expressions of concern. *"Away up here in snowbound North Dakota we have been listening in on flood reports from your city and wish to add our little bit to relieve the suffering and distress,"* was one message received by WHAS. From Lille, France, a small boy sent his donation of 14 francs.

Cleanup continued for many months following the recession of the waters. A massive civic program of restoration of streets, sidewalks, utilities and equipment was necessary. With the help of the federal government, Louisville was able to rebuild its civil services and make improvements in many areas.

The city's goal was to restore streets and sewer services by Derby Day in May. Ground water welling up into sewers made the work difficult, uncomfortable and dangerous. Repairman Tom Kessinger raced up a ladder from a shaft at Fourth and Liberty when gasoline ignited and shot flames 60 feet in the air.

The paddock area of Churchill Downs is usually pictured hosting thousands of celebrating race fans. Covered in water, the familiar race track scene becomes an eerie and frightening environment. Visitors to the 1937 Derby were amazed that all signs of destruction had been erased from the historic track, and Churchill Downs was back to its normal high standards of excellence.

1937 Ohio River Flood Photograph Collections – 1986.71.03

Churchill Downs became a major relief station for African–Americans during the Flood. For ten days, the sick and injured were treated at the track and housed in the luxurious dining room. The U.S. Army provided blankets and cots, and a refugee dormitory was set up in the elegant mirrored restaurant.

1937 Ohio River Flood Photograph Collections (Corwin Short Photos) – 2002.010.020

Kessinger grinned when he philosophically described his narrow escape, "That was just one of those things that happen."

Like most natural disasters, the 1937 Flood provided economic benefit for some. Through the WPA, CCC and other governmental agencies, many new jobs were created during the cleanup campaign. The Standard Printing Company earned over a half–million dollars from cleaning and drying books and papers and publishing souvenir post cards. Low interest government loans helped many small businessmen re-establish themselves and improve their opportunities.

First–time visitors to the Kentucky Derby are often surprised to discover that the famous Churchill Downs racetrack is so near downtown. Virtually the entire track was water–covered, except for small elevated areas near Shed Row on the backside. Although Central Avenue was navigable in February, by May the great thoroughbred War Admiral would race to victory on a track described as fast.

R.G. Potter Collection – 522

Dirty Money

J. A. Schacht, cashier at the Federal Reserve Bank, supervised in one of the strangest rites of cleanup after the Flood. Waterlogged cash and mud-covered coins from banks in Jeffersonville, New Albany and Paducah required cleaning. He and his staff washed the mud off $10,000 in nickels, dimes and quarters. About $50,000 in cash was placed in large, flat pans and placed in stoves for drying.

When the cash was dry enough to be separated, each individual bill was pressed with an electric iron. Due to the danger from infection, the cash did not go back into circulation, but was systematically sliced in two, with one part going back to Washington for replacement, and the other half serving as a receipt until the money was replaced.

The Red Cross, having already done so much, was on hand during the aftermath to help individuals get back on their feet. While they did not provide assistance to businesses, they did assist small one-person enterprises. A woman cobbler had her small shop and equipment donated by the Red Cross, as did a music teacher who was given a free piano.

Despite the heroic work done by local police, after the flood there were allegations of whiskey and beer in the stations, a direct violation of official policy. Captain Walter Smith, commander of the First District Police station, readily admitted in a hearing that during the flood he drank only beer, because he felt the water was not safe. He also admitted that he and some of his men shared a bottle of whiskey because such a stimulant was needed by the men on duty. The hearing officers of his review board agreed.

A few months later, another review board took harsher measures by firing three officers. Patrolman Glen D. Shomate was charged with inefficiency and conduct unbecoming an officer. Robert P. Merritt failed to report for duty to his superiors, and Edward Noone took his family to the East End for safety and failed to return to the West End. He claimed to have been marooned and unable to report for duty. Safety Director Wakefield rejected their appeals: *"In view of our having to ask other cities for police help, we cannot condone absence or laxity on the part of our own men."*

In the first full month following the Ohio River flood, Louisville retailing was 40.6 percent above the same month of the previous year. The national average was about 10 percent. Collection of taxes and payments on installment plans remained at normal levels. One of the city's large department stores had approximately 1,000 installment accounts on appliances located in the flooded areas. Only one of their customers refused payment on her ruined refrigerator and demanded the store repossess the appliance.

Louisville did not lose a single industry due to the Flood, and shortly afterwards the Bernheim distilling plant was purchased by Schenley Distillers for $22,000,000. An out-of-town corporation which had been considering moving to Louisville reported that the flood had increased its admiration for the fine community spirit that had been manifested.

The Flood significantly changed patterns of living for Louisvillians. People became discouraged over persistent flooding in low-lying areas and began to build their homes

The Velvet Racer, the grand wooden roller–coaster at Fontaine Ferry Park, was destroyed when a floating house was swept into the amusement ride. Over 50 refugees who retreated to Fontaine Ferry remained throughout the crisis. Damaged like all other West End structures, the beloved amusement park was restored and re–opened within a few months of the Flood.

1937 Ohio River Flood Photograph Collections (Corwin Short Photos) – 2002.010.040

further from the Ohio River. Many families began looking to the city's East End, or the comparative safety of rural Jefferson County. St. Matthews changed from potato farms to suburban center. In 1938, the City of Shively was incorporated, and so many West End families moved to the area that it became known as "New Portland."

During Derby Week of 1937, city fathers proudly announced a major new roads project to be completed before the next Derby. The roads, intended to facilitate a more effective evacuation plan, included: a divided four–lane road between Middletown and Louisville; a two–lane section of U.S. 42 between the Zachary Taylor Monument and the Oldham County line, completing the highway link to Cincinnati; repaving and adding a railroad overpass on Seventh Street Road from Berry Boulevard to St. Helens; reconstruction of

the Preston Street Road from Louisville to the Bullitt County line; and reconstruction of 18th Street Road (Dixie Highway) to St. Helens.

After the crisis came a time for assessment and appraisal. It was determined that the most successful of all businesses during the crisis was the Western Union Telegraph Company. Telegraph service provided the fastest way to send and receive written messages in the days before faxes and e–mails. Located at Fourth and Market, Western Union stood upon the dry ground that was the island of downtown Louisville. G.L. Musick, superintendent, reported they handled 415,254 messages and delivered $75,000 in cash to their customers.

When the river first reached flood stage the company rushed 105 employees to Louisville to assist the local office. They prepared for emergency power by installing two power plants, operated by automobile motors. When the regular electrical power was lost, Western Union was down only five minutes before their backup system was started. It was the only interruption they experienced throughout the crisis.

Western Union understood about planning ahead. To provide for their employees, both local and special out–of–town help, the firm brought into Louisville a relief train with 13 sleeping, dining, water and provision cars.

The shared flood experience helped establish a new city in terms of social attitudes. Often for the first time, "West Enders" came to know and respect "East Enders". Fate had put them in the same boat and they began to recognize their fellowship. Bridges were built between races as well. Inspiring examples of cooperation, caring and respect were witnessed between white and black citizens. Despite the conflicting traditions of Louisville's heritage, both midwestern and southern in viewpoint, a new contract of understanding was being negotiated.

Mayor Miller, as so often was the case, articulated the important lessons to be gained from the shared flood experience. *"There is much to make history in Louisville in those friendships which were built up when the rich and poor labored side–by–side to rescue their fellow–men, when executive and truck driver jointly operated a truck in carrying food to the homeless, when Protestant, Catholic and Jew filled sand bags to protect the homes of those they had never before seen….I think we shall all thank God that we live in a city which has shown the resourcefulness to meet the catastrophe, the generosity to take care of the weak and helpless, and the determination to work together for a greater Louisville."*

The Flood's crest is marked by an oil slick as the river recedes. The sign board of the Shawnee Branch of the First National Bank provides a graphic reminder of the highest peak of flooding, and a clear indication of how much water remained. Houses, buildings, telephone poles and signs all over Louisville bore tell–tale high water marks.

Mayor's Scrapbook – page 40

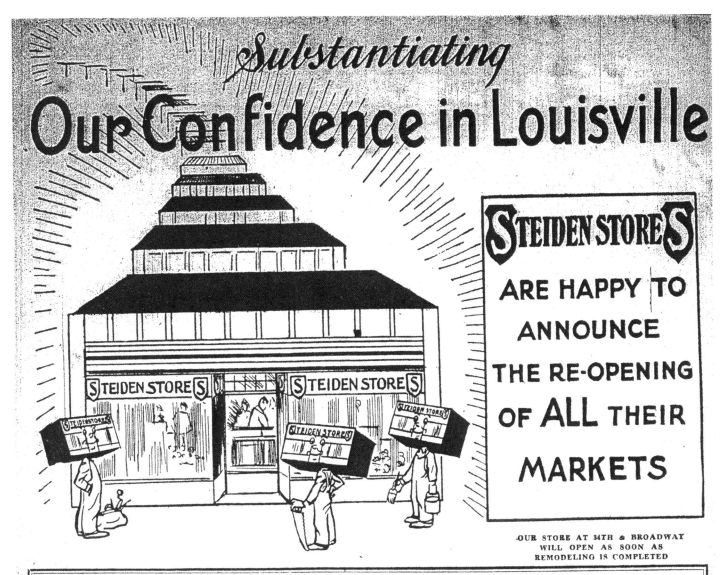

Substantiating
Our Confidence in Louisville

STEIDEN STORES
ARE HAPPY TO
ANNOUNCE
THE RE-OPENING
OF ALL THEIR
MARKETS

OUR STORE AT 34TH & BROADWAY
WILL OPEN AS SOON AS
REMODELING IS COMPLETED

A REAL VALUE IN QUALITY SHORTENING			
FOR FRYING OR COOKING	**SNOWDRIFT**	2-LB. CAN	**30**c
SCHOOL DAYS	**PEAS**	NO. 2 CAN	**10**c
IVORY WHITE	**SOAP**	MEDIUM BAR (LG. BAR 10c)	**5**½c

Caufield & Shook
Louisville

The Western Union Telegraph Company's office at Fourth and Market streets was well–prepared for the disaster and handled record numbers of communications and cash transfers. The company shipped in hundreds of extra workers, and gasoline–powered generators, to maintain vital communication services.

Small Groups Collection – 1984.01.03

Henry Clay Weeden was a remarkable man for his time, or any time. He began life as a slave, but would grow up to become a scholar, writer, historian, preacher and educator. Born in 1862, he died in October 1937, just eight months after the flood. Active in post–Civil War Republican politics, he rose to a high position with the post office. In 1897 he wrote *Weeden's History of the Colored People of Louisville*, the seminal historical study of the city's African–American community. Weeks after the crest of the flood, H. C. Weeden wrote the following letter to the editor of the *Courier–Journal*.

Sometimes for the first time, black and white Louisvillians were brought together through their shared experience during the 1937 Flood. African-American children, and their families, were housed and fed in the elegant Churchill Down's dining room during the unparalleled crisis of community need.

*1937 Ohio River Flood Photograph Collections
(Corwin Short Photos) – 2002.010.027*

LETTER TO THE EDITOR
GRATEFUL COLORED PEOPLE

As a long time citizen here, from boyhood days, I am able to speak with authority. I know of the good association and cooperation that the white people have given to the colored people in this city, how they have taken part in such affairs to advance their interests socially, morally and religiously.

I recall the time when the Colored Orphan's Home held its first meeting in Doctor Humphrey's church, corner Second and College Streets, and the next meeting was held in the Second Presbyterian Church, Second and Broadway.

I want to say with pleasure and delight and I congratulate the white people for the unlimited interest shown my people in this last great calamity, the flood, which overshadowed our city, and the way in which our people were removed to places of safety. How they visited our homes and got them in boats through the water.

I do not think there is any city outside of Louisville whose class of white people will equal or surpass those of our city and I am quite sure that I can speak in behalf of all the colored people in the city when I say that we are grateful for all the efforts made in our behalf, in this time of trouble.

I am speaking from personal observation, since my daughter and I were carried across the water in a boat and landed at Barret and Broadway, and I remained there until dusk in order that I might personally observe as to how things were managed and conducted. It was a wonderful job and all races and persons, no discrimination being shown as to race, color or previous servitude, were considered.

H. C. Weeden
Louisville

WHAS Radio hosted a civic celebration at the Jefferson County Armory (now Louisville Gardens) to thank the public for their efforts. Fifteen thousand Louisvillians streamed into the Jefferson County Armory on February 16 to enjoy a civic gala of survival. Vaudeville acts and local musicians shared the stage with politicians and community leaders to hear updates on the events of the recent past. The crowd grew into a swelling chorus when led in a rendition of "My Old Kentucky Home." The song's nostalgic melancholy rang especially true for this generation of Kentuckians.

Mayor Miller offered his hardy review of the city's condition. He reported no epidemics, no increase in disease, very few drowning victims and no unidentified bodies. All large commercial structures were sound and the streets were cleaned. Ambassador Robert W. Bingham, freshly returned from England, offered his sage observations. "We are humbly proud, but deeply proud, that we are part of a people whose fiber stood the test of flood as it did. The flood has drawn our city and state closer together…I think that out of all this is coming understanding, an essential community of interest, that will mean much to the future."

Rabbi Joseph Rauch praised "the Unknown Soldiers of the flood" – the utility workers and man on the street – "who worked as men have never worked before." The WHAS Show and Celebration, a combination of local entertainment, fundraising and civic pride, almost certainly served as a model for the subsequent WHAS Crusade for Children program that continues today.

The Mayor's Committee on Morale had served throughout the crisis by encouraging positive attitudes and endorsed good old-fashioned American boosterism. Following the Flood, they printed and distributed orange pledge cards to be pinned to lapels and coats. "I will do my part toward building a better and greater Louisville", the cards declared. "I Dare You To Catch Me Not Smiling" was the bold tag line on the boosters' badges.

The Jefferson County Armory (today's Louisville Gardens) was a haven of rest and assistance to over 75,000 citizens during the crisis. Boredom, disorder and close proximity were stressful to adults and children alike. In 1937, the County Armory cared for more than three times the number of refugees who crowded the Superdome during the Hurricane Katrina disaster of 2005.

LG&E workers labored in the Beargrass Substation to dry and clean every machine needed to restore normal power to the city. Officials from the Louisville Water Company and LG&E made major structural adjustments to their plants to guard against future flooding.

Caufield and Shook Collection – 149645

Pin this on your coat

MY PLEDGE

I will not complain.

I will not spread bad news.

I will be encouraging, helpful, friendly.

I will work unselfishly.

I will give all I can.

I will do my part toward building a better and a greater LOUISVILLE

— AND —

I Dare You To Catch Me Not Smiling

— Mayor's Committee on Morale —

The First Saturday in May Sees a Fast Track

The 1937 Derby Festival Parade, also called the Carnival Night Parade at that time, was held on Fourth Street rather than on Broadway as it is today. The street, completely inundated just three months earlier, was clean, dry, and packed with thousands of enthusiastic individuals who were glad to celebrate after so much hardship.

Courier-Journal

Within a few months of the Flood, Derby Day visitors were amazed the city had recovered so completely. Much of the famed racetrack Churchill Downs had been submerged under six feet of water. The upper floor restaurant had served as a refuge station for African–Americans and an oil stain marked the high water location on all the painted white structures.

By the first Saturday in May, Louisville put the welcome mat out and all necessary repairs had been made. A crowd of 70,000 watched War Admiral, a son of Man O' War, win the race in a time of 2:03 1/5. The track condition was officially listed as fast – not muddy.

The City of Louisville made adjustments in urban planning. Shippingport was dismantled, with only a handful of old fishermen returning to their former town site. In 1958, even these few individuals were removed. The city also used the opportunity to improve sanitation and sewage systems, and soon outdoor privies became a thing of the past in Louisville.

Mayor Miller saw the aftermath of the Flood as an opportunity to enhance public services and he chose Derby Week, with thousands of visitors, to publish his assessment. He reported that all services had been restored to pre–flood normalcy, or better. Collection of taxes remained normal and produced adequate revenue to pay for all regular governmental services. The immunization of hundreds of thousands of citizens against typhoid fever would continue to protect them for years to come. Most of the dwellings destroyed by flood waters were old, unsafe and unsanitary and were not up to contemporary standards. Miller cited that sanitary conditions and fire protection had improved, as had the appearance of the city's neighborhoods. For the first time, one–way streets were instituted to accommodate a growing number of personal vehicles.

Caufield and Shook Collection – 149495

R.G. Potter Collection – 5980

Caufield and Shook Collection – 149779

Mayor Miller proposed to de–populate the low–lying Point and Portland Wharf areas and replace the frequently–destroyed areas with public parks and recreational areas. The Point would become the future home of a string of beautiful riverside parks running from downtown's Waterfront Park to River Road's Cox Park. George A. Droppelman, a member of the Portland Civic Club, urged passage of the amendment to level the old Portland wharf area. "A city is no more beautiful than its ugliest spot," opined Droppelman.

The Louisville Water Company and LG&E embarked on ambitious programs to make their facilities safer from flooding. Buildings were raised and entrances sealed to avoid duplication of the recent disaster. To signal LG&E's commitment to its customers, president T. Bert Wilson decreed that neither he nor any of his executives would utilize the fully–operational lamps on their desks until electrical power was restored to every residential customer. For weeks, LG&E officials worked at their desks using old–fashioned kerosene lamps.

Recognizing the critical role played by airplane loads of emergency supplies, Mayor Miller pledged improvement to Bowman Field's runways and other facilities.

Following the Second World War, the U.S. Government and the Army Corps of Engineers began an elaborate and expensive system of flood walls and levees, along with reservoirs to help contain the Ohio River's waters. Beginning in 1947, the government spent millions of dollars to design and build over 29 miles of floodwalls and levees in Jefferson County. The floodwalls are designed to control flooding by standing three feet higher than the 1937 crest. This ambitious flood control system was built by the Army Corps of Engineers and is maintained and operated by the Metropolitan Sewer District.

The utter devastation in the Point neighborhood spurred city officials to raze the area and permanently relocate the residents. Houses and buildings on Adams Street were piled upon each other, making reconstruction impossible. Three small shotgun houses on River Road, near the Cut–Off Bridge, were tumbled by the current and rolled onto their sides. Structures careened into the supports of the Big Four Bridge and were destroyed. Louisville officials vowed to make improvements, and today the Point has been transformed into Waterfront Park, and other recreational areas.

"…the Flood made you all better neighbors."

President Franklin D. Roosevelt

One of the peculiar aspects of the 1937 Flood was its extreme longevity. Most natural disasters – earthquakes, tornados, fire and even floods – are of relatively short duration. They come and go quickly and leave their damage behind. In Louisville, the river remained above flood stage for 18 consecutive days, and many areas were seriously affected before the normal flood stage was even reached.

Remarkably, throughout all the danger, discomfort and fear, people found the courage to laugh. In years to come, in drier and warmer times, people traded stories of their mistakes, foolishness or accidents. Friends reminded their pals of falling out of boats, fishing out of second story windows, or losing their good luck piece. With the passage of time, lessons learned from the 1937 Flood were often passed along as self–deprecating jokes, or wry observations of those dangerous times.

Fortunately, among the pictures of distress and suffering there will always be many of the opposite kind, spreading widely abroad humor, optimism, joy and genuine satisfaction. Here is the abrupt, the laughable overturning of an unsteady skiff, boat or canoe in shallow water at point of landing; there the bright and cheerful faces and voices of the sturdy rescuers as some house top or porch roof is finally unloaded of its human freight. Who can forget those glad, those joyous cries and many happy tears as the juvenile members of families once separated are again united. These and a thousand similar scenes will be told and retold in Louisville as years pass by and the eventful days of the great flood of 1937 are recalled. They are of the kind of stuff the heart never forgets!

The GREAT FLOOD of 1937 in LOUISVILLE, KENTUCKY
By Willard Rouse Jillson

Remarkably, throughout the Flood, people took the Committee on Morale's advice and kept smiling. Three friends wade through water–covered Logan Street, between Kentucky and Breckinridge, and show little concern for their circumstances. Rubber boots, one of the most prized possessions during the Flood, perhaps added to their sense of well–being.

R.G. Potter Collection – 6541

Standard Oil employees enjoy a moment of fun during a break in their rescue work. The friendships made, and memories shared, have been some of the most enduring legacies of the Great Flood of 1937. An enhanced sense of community helped Louisville, and neighboring towns, recover from their challenges.

Collection of Scott Nussbaum

The jaunty crew of a whiskey–barrel raft, commanded by Louis C. Haungs (standing), negotiates the inundated corner of Fourth and Gaulbert streets. A sense of adventure pervaded the community, and for decades people looked back and remembered humorous experiences during their trial.

Caufield and Shook Collection – 149484 1/2

When the emergency stage was over, public recognition of significant contributions commenced. WHAS received the Columbia Award for Distinguished Contribution to the Radio Art by William S. Paley, president of CBS. Previous winners of the award included Charles Lindbergh, Amelia Earhart, Leopold Stokowsky, Nino Martini and Rear Admiral Richard E. Byrd. WHAS was the first radio station to receive the honor.

Barry Bingham, Sr. accepted the award and expressed Louisville's gratitude to the outside world. He described the "feeling of cold isolation" that had affected Louisvillians when they thought they were cut off from the world.

"Then, in the midst of feverish rescue work, our people began to realize that Louisville was not cut off from the outside world, but rather that people all over the United States were sharing our difficulties and straining every resource to help us. Help began to pour in…It was then that we began to realize the great power of radio. The great, generous heart of America opened to the suffering of our community…Louisville suffered a disaster, but Louisville found millions of friends through that disaster. We will never forget them."

"The Heritage of Undying Experiences"

Many public officials and workers deserved recognition for their dedication to duty and the selflessness of their work. Workers in the LG&E generating plants and the Louisville Water Company pumping stations risked their lives to keep their operations functioning. Firemen and police officers worked unending hours in the worst imaginable conditions. Telephone workers – operators, engineers and linemen – were valiant and dedicated to their commitment to keep lines of communication open. Doctors, nurses and other medical professionals labored under terrible circumstances to maintain the public health. Journalists rose to new standards of excellence and dedication to the public good. To Mayor Neville Miller, and his administration, the city will always be beholden for their ennobling of the term "civil servant." Untold numbers of men and women worked together to save their community.

When Margaret Bourke–White's portrait of Uncle Jim Lawhorn appeared in *LIFE* magazine, the 90 year–old ex–slave became a national celebrity. Lawson, of 2908 South Sixth Street, spent ten days in the Churchill Downs dining room where he was photographed. A lady from Tacoma, Washington was moved by the elderly gentleman's dignity in the face of disaster, and mailed him a five dollar bill. Upon receiving the gift, Mr. Lawson replied, "This is a lot of money. I would like to thank that nice lady," he said. "Religion and money are the greatest things in the world."

1937 Ohio River Flood Photograph Collections (Corwin Short Photos) – 2002.010.023

Remembrance of the Great Flood of 1937 in Louisville, Kentucky, will remain as long as life persists in the bodies of those whose loved ones and property were imperiled by it. On–the–spot observers, those to whom fickle circumstances were kind or unkind as the case may have been, will never forget! Even children hardly able to toddle at their parents' side during the great lowland exodus will in a dim but certain way recall, when as much as four score years and more shall have passed, the distress, the panic, the horror of it all. Down the widely ramifying paths of life of the countless thousands who were helplessly caught in the fateful grasp of this great natural catastrophe will do scenes of human misery and suffering, hundreds of them, the heritage of undying experiences. In all of these pictures of the battle to save life against frightful odds will remain the gaunt specter of cold, bone–chilling, damp cold; hunger, growing and insatiable; sickness, despair and death.

The GREAT FLOOD of 1937 in LOUISVILLE, KENTUCKY
By Willard Rouse Jillson

"Janitor to Lie in State"

The body of Thomas Mac Avaney, Negro, 55, janitor at the Highland Presbyterian Church, 1001 Cherokee Rd., will lie in state at the church from 11 a.m. until 1 p.m. Thursday. He died at 8 p.m. Monday at the City Hospital following a heart attack.

His body will be taken at 1 p.m. to the Lampton Baptist Church, 528 S. Hancock St., where Dr. P. H. Pluene, pastor of the Highland Presbyterian Church, and the Rev. J. M. Williams, Negro, pastor of the Lampton Baptist Church, will conduct services.

Dr. Plune said Mac Avaney spent thirteen sleepless days and nights helping care for 300 flood refugees at the Highland Church.

Mac Avaney lived in the rear of 921 Baxter Ave. He is survived by his wife, Mary Jane Mac Avaney.

Courier–Journal
February 17, 1937

The Flooded Area as shown hereon was determined from actual field observations being made by the ENGINEERING DEPARTMENT of the COMMISSIONERS of SEWERAGE of Louisville

FLOOD of LOUISVILLE

CREST OF FLOOD JAN

OFFICIAL READING OF CREST AT

Elev. 460

(RIVER GAUGE 57.4 FE

COPYRIGHT FEBRUARY 1
THE STANDARD PRINTE
INCORPORATED
LOUISVILLE, KENTUC
U. S. A.

KEY TO FLOOD DATA ON MAP
RED NUMBERS INDICATE APPROXIMATE DEPTH OF WATER IN FEET AT THAT POINT. BLUE INDICATES FLOODED AREA. ★ ★ ★ ★

NORMAL POOL (LOUISVILLE) DAM No. 41 IS ELEV. 420.0.
PAVEMENT AT 4th and CHESTNUT ELEV. 459.0.
FRANKFORT AVE. AT CRESTMORE IN CRESCENT HILL ELEV. 550.0 APPROX.
All Elevations given refer to Sea Level Datum.

CORRECT FLOOD INFORMATION ON THIS SECTION IS NOT AVAILABLE

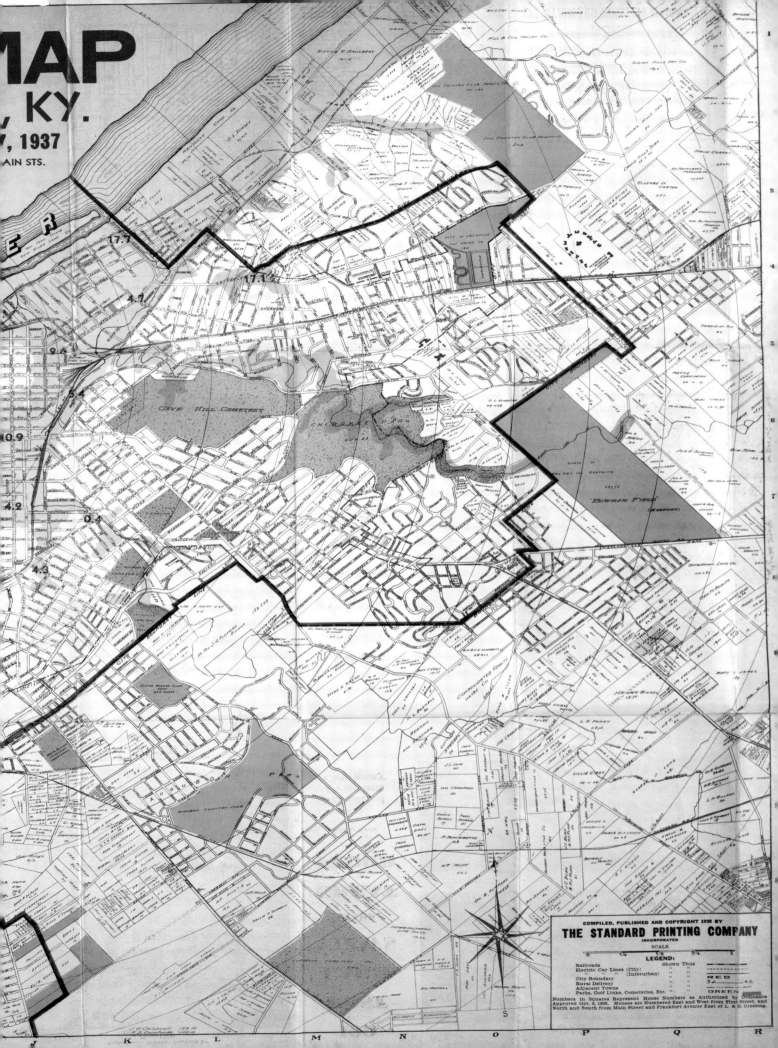

CAVE HILL CEMETERY

CHEROKEE PARK

BOWMAN FIELD
(AIRPORT)

AUDUBON PARK

AUDUBON COUNTRY CLUB

COMPILED, PUBLISHED AND COPYRIGHT 1936 BY
THE STANDARD PRINTING COMPANY
INCORPORATED
SCALE

LEGEND:

Railroads .... Shown Thus
Electric Car Lines (City) ....
            (Interurban) ...
City Boundary ....
Rural Delivery ....
Adjacent Towns ....
Parks, Golf Links, Cemeteries, Etc.

Numbers in Squares Represent House Numbers as Authorized by Ordinance
Approved Oct. 2, 1905. Houses are Numbered East and West from First Street, and
North and South from Main Street and Frankfort Avenue East of L. & N. Crossing.

From the disastrous '37 Flood, enduring photographic images recall the horrors, and triumphs, experienced during the crisis.

1937 Ohio River Flood Photograph Collections — 1986.65.06

A refugee walks the one–way Pontoon Bridge to safety; and a stark tree in Shawnee Park reflects its image upon standing waters that challenged, but could not destroy, its home.

1937 Ohio River Flood Photograph Collections (Corwin Short Photos) – 2002.010.006

"We will build a better and a greater Louisville."

Mayor Neville Miller

In the final analysis, the most important monument of the 1937 Flood does not lie in high water markers on buildings or the civic improvements which emerged. The legacy of the 1937 Flood is the spirit exemplified in the words of Louisville's Great Flood Mayor, Neville Miller:

"This flood has shown how weak is man; in a day, the waters have covered our city, extinguished our lights, flooded our homes, stopped our factories – closed our schools, our churches, and our courts… The flood has also shown us how strong we are. In this disaster, comparatively few of our people have perished; our hearts and our purses, our homes have been open and we have found a strength we did not know we possessed… We will build a better and a greater Louisville. The city is not built of brick and mortar, not of wood and stone alone: it is built of, as it is being built by, the men and women who inhabit it."

"Louisville Marches On"

Courier–Journal Editorial Cartoon, February 16, 1937

HONOR TO WHOM HONOR IS DUE

by Dr. George Ferris Payne, 1937

We never shall forget the flood
Of nineteen–thirty–seven;
Which gave so many people,
One–Way–Tickets straight to Heaven.

A lot of others got free rides,
To places near and far;
Now relatives are wondering,
Just where on earth they are.

The Red Cross took them in their boats,
To havens here and there;
Then gave them shelter, food and clothes,
And every other care.

We ought to sing the praises,
Of the Red Cross every day;
And also of the workers
Of the W.P.A.

Police from other cities,
Should receive their share of praise
For help, aid and assistance,
In so many different ways.

We certainly feel grateful,
And to them we tender thanks,
For helping us until the flood,
Got back within its banks.

To all Boy Scouts of Louisville,
And every Legionnaire,
We owe a debt of gratitude
For help in our despair.

A lot of other agencies
(I cannot name them all).
Gave clothing, food and shelter
In response to every call.

The noblest of our heroes,
Have been overlooked, I guess;
The radio announcing boys
Of W.H.A.S.

All honor to those gallant lads,
Who labored day and night;
Exhausted, yet they carried on,
Until they won the fight.

Their messages brought prompt relief
To thousands in distress;
So let us not forget the boys,
Of W.H.A.S.

They saved the lives of many,
There can be no doubt of that;
And for these noble services,
To them we doff our hat.

T'is only right and proper;
That all honor and all praise,
Be tendered those who helped so much,
Through all those hectic days.

In closing may I say just this,
Now that the flood is gone;
As true Kentuckians we shall see,
That "Louisville Marches On."

ABOUT THE AUTHOR

RICK BELL, Executive Director of the U.S. Marine Hospital Foundation, is a native of the Portland neighborhood in Louisville, Kentucky. A non-profit fundraising professional for over 30 years, Bell attended the University of Kentucky where he majored in journalism. He was awarded two Photographic Department internships at Louisville's *Courier-Journal.*

Formerly the Assistant to the Director of The Filson Club in Louisville, Bell and his wife Susie designed the Museum of The Filson Club and operated their own museum exhibit design firm. Among their projects were the Nature Center for the Indiana Dunes State Park and the Kennedy Southwestern Collection at Ohio University.

Experts in folk art and Navajo weaving, they lived in southwestern Colorado for 10 years, returning to Louisville in 2001. While living at the base of Mesa Verde National Park, Bell provided photographs for five books and operated Folk Art of the Four Corners Gallery, the nation's only Navajo folk art retailer. Bell also worked at Crow Canyon Archaeological Center and served as Interim Executive Director of the Gallup Intertribal Indian Ceremonial, the nation's oldest and largest Indian arts festival.

He is married to Susie Campbell Bell, a faculty member of Louisville Design Tech and an interior designer. The Bells, their cat Petoskey, and two Golden Retrievers now live in Louisville's Crescent Hill neighborhood.

Cover   *Caufield and Shook Collection – 149513*

Page 5   Bailing out their car with a coffee pot produced laughter for (left to right) Minerva Simpson, Mrs. J. P. Monks and Mrs. W. F. Diebold. The photo was taken in front of Miss Simpson's home at 4614 W. Broadway, near the entrance of Shawnee Park.
1937 Ohio River Flood Photograph Collections – 1993.25.03

Back Cover   *R.G. Potter Collection – 3435.2*